# THE BEST OF

*The A.R.E.*
## JOURNAL

# THE BEST OF

# *The A.R.E.* JOURNAL

**Compiled by
Ken Skidmore**

ARE
PRESS

**ASSOCIATION FOR
RESEARCH AND
ENLIGHTENMENT**

A.R.E. Press • Virginia Beach • Virginia

A.R.E. Press
215 67th Street
Virginia Beach, VA 23451-2061

The articles in this book are reprinted from *The A.R.E. Journal*, copyright 1970 to 1977 by the Association for Research and Enlightenment, Inc. They are reprinted as originally published with only slight editorial modification where necessary for factual correction. The Edgar Cayce readings are quoted as originally published in these articles and may vary slightly from the *Edgar Cayce Readings CD-ROM* due to author editing.

The best of the A.R.E. journal / compiled by Ken Skidmore.
    p.    cm.
Includes bibliographical references.
ISBN 0-87604-430-5 (trade pbk.)
1. Association for Research and Enlightenment—Doctrines.
I. Title: Best of the Association for Research and Enlightenment journal. II. Skidmore, Ken, 1944- III. A.R.E. journal.

BP605.A77 B47    2000
133.8—dc21

                                    00-045121

Cover design by Richard Boyle

# Contents

# Introction

THE EDGAR CAYCE psychic readings have been helping people for a hundred years now, since the first reading that Edgar Cayce gave for himself. Initially the information was only available to those who actually received the readings. As the body of Cayce's work grew, though, others wished to benefit first from the physical information and later from the spiritual information. The need for published material became apparent.

The history of A.R.E. publications goes back to before the Association for Research and Enlightenment, Inc., (A.R.E.) actually existed! In the late 1920s, the Association of National Investigators (A.N.I.) was the precursor of the A.R.E., which was founded by Edgar Cayce in 1931. Tom Sugrue, who would later write Edgar Cayce's biography, *There Is a River*, was the editor of an A.N.I. journal called *The New Tomorrow*, which published articles based on Edgar Cayce's psychic insights. Over thirty-five years later, after many smaller publications such as the *Searchlight* and the *Bulletin* were tried, another journal, *The A.R.E. Journal*, was begun.

*The A.R.E. Journal* was published from 1966 until 1984, when the *Venture Inward* magazine was formed. The *Journal* was intended as a vehicle for both academic articles and for popular ones covering all aspects of the Cayce material. Studies done in the Association's research department in Virginia Beach, Virginia, or at the A.R.E. Clinic in Phoenix, Arizona, or elsewhere were reported in those pages. Hugh Lynn Cayce's trips to the Holy Land and Egypt were described to our members. New discoveries concerning Atlantis at Bimini in the Bahamas were released to the readership. Each issue featured an inspirational look at principles from the readings, as well.

Many of the authors published in the *Journal* were lecturers around the country, and some later went on to write books. Some were well known in their fields before writing for the *Journal*. All in all, *The A.R.E. Journal* published quite a variety of thought-provoking articles in those eighteen years. I had the pleasure of being the editor of that publication for the last eight years of its life and have had the opportunity to compile this collection.

This reprise of some of the best of the material from the '70s is primarily focused on aspects of spiritual growth, from concepts of reincarnation to principles found in the Search for God groups. Additionally, there are short pieces on subjects ranging from business ideals to the importance of music in one's life. It is hoped that readers will find inspirational material here to reacquaint them with the basic spiritual principles in their lives.

Those long familiar with the psychic readings of Edgar Cayce will find reminders of the strong spiritual message that first attracted them to this information. Those new to the Cayce concepts will find helpful overviews of many of the wonderful insights contained in the readings. This is a book that can be handed to anyone looking for answers to life's many questions.

Over the years that I worked with the *Journal*, one of my great pleasures was reading the wealth of helpful spiritual guidance that authors plucked from the Cayce readings. Working with one's dreams, watching one's diet, meditating on a daily basis are all manageable tasks that can be integrated into a seeker's life. So, there is a practical side to this volume of articles, as well. The philosophical truths presented here are meant to be applied.

I trust that each reader will leave this volume of articles with that nugget of truth that will turn ordinary moments into hopeful times of spiritual growth.

Ken Skidmore
November 2000

# Successful Living

## by Warren C. Propes

*(Q) Please advise the body as to how he may best gain control of himself and utilize his abilities to an advantage.*

(A) Depend more upon the intuitive forces from within and not harken so much to that of outside influences but learn to listen to that still small voice from within, remembering the lesson as was given: not in the storm, the lightning, nor in any of the loud noises as are made to attract men, but rather in the still small voice from within does the impelling influence come to life in an individual that gives for that which must be the basis of human endeavor; for without the ability to constantly hold before self the ideal as is attempted to be accomplished, man be-

**comes as one adrift, pulled hither and yon by the various calls and cries of those who would give of this world's pleasure in fame, fortune, or what not. Let these be the outcome of a life spent in listening to the divine from within, and not the purpose of the life. 239-1**

Here we find success defined very differently from the way we usually think of it. Many conceive of success only in the material sense—fame, riches, a multitude of friends, and public esteem. To others success comes with peace of mind, security, and love. How acceptable are these goals? How can life be made more meaningful? In short, how can we become successful? Cayce could give no easy answer to these questions, for the solution to this problem, as with most problems, is within ourselves. Hence, each individual must seek the answer himself through prayer, meditation, and a search for his ideal.

Prayer gives us purpose, energy, and a pathway to our goal. So to obtain success, however we define it, prayer is necessary. Dr. Alexis Carrel regards prayer as an emanation from man's worshiping spirit, the release of powerful energy which gives an increase of physical buoyancy, intellectual vigor, moral stamina, and a deeper understanding of the realities underlying human relationships. How does prayer help us to achieve our purpose? Prayer puts into force the principle of action. It is doubtful if one could pray for fulfillment day after day without doing something about it.

In the meditation chapter of *A Search for God,* we find prayer defined:

"Prayer is the concerted effort of our physical consciousness to become attuned to the Consciousness of the Creator. It is the attunement of our conscious minds to the spiritual forces that manifest in a material world. It may be a cooperative experience of many individuals, coming together with one accord and with one mind."

This definition of prayer is much more profound than the dictionary one of "Thanks and praise given to God, and requests made of Him." The Cayce readings define prayer as a mental, physical, and spiritual experience. It is not just an entreaty or a supplication; it is an attunement with our Creator. We seek to become one with God and to be perfect as our Father in Heaven is perfect.

" . . . coming together with one accord and with one mind" refers, of course, to group prayer, which has long been considered the most effective prayer. The Indian *Vedas*, thousands of years ago, taught that any two people, uniting their psychic forces, could conquer the world. *For where two or three are gathered together in my name, there am I in the midst of them.* (Matt. 18:20) In this connection, the readings not only recommend the use of study groups for self-development but also suggest church attendance.

**Do not get away from the church! In the church keep those activities, that there may be a surety in self, that has to do or to deal with only the use of such insight, such vision, to the glory of the Father as manifested in the Son. 4087-1**

When the question was asked about what church one should join, the answer was:

**Remember, rather, the church is within self. As to the organization, choose that—not as a convenience for thee, but where ye may serve the better, whatever its name—let it be thy life proclaiming Jesus the Christ. 3342-1**

In what way is prayer related to our ideal? Martin Luther, a very practical man, stated: "Whatever then the heart clings to and relies upon, that is properly thy God." Proverbs 23:7 tells us: *For as he thinketh in his heart, so is he.* We must keep our ideal high, for unspiritualized forces can do great damage. Revelation 13 shows the great power of selfish and misdirected energy. Tyrants frequently boast they are God-inspired, and such a statement leave many confused and helpless. *And they worshipped the dragon which gave power unto the beast: and they worshipped the beast, saying Who is like unto the beast? Who is able to make war with him?* (Rev. 13:4) How can we avoid this entrapment in our search for a meaningful life?

Repeat three times every day, and then listen:

**"Lord, what wouldst Thou have me do today?"** **Do not do this as rote. Mean it! . . . 3303-1**

The second key to self-development is meditation. *A Search for God* defines meditation as:

" . . . the emptying of ourselves of all that hinders the Creative Force from rising along the natural channels of our physical bodies to be disseminated through the sensitive spiritual centers in our physical bodies . . . In prayer we speak to God, in meditation God speaks to us."

This seems to indicate a passive state, yet the rewards obtained from meditation have been rich experiences, inexpressibly beautiful.

"St. Ignatius confessed one day to Father Laynez that a single hour of meditation at Manresa had taught him more truths about heavenly things than all the teachings of all the doctors put together could have taught him . . . One day in orison [prayer] on the steps of the choir of the Dominican Church, he saw in a distinct manner the plan of divine wisdom in the creation of the world. On another occasion, during a procession, his spirit was ravished in God, and it was given him to contemplate, in a form and images fitted to the weak understanding of a dweller on earth, the deep mystery of the Holy Trinity. This last vision flooded his heart with such sweetness, that the mere memory of it in after times made him shed abundant tears." (William James, *The Varieties of Religious Experience*)

Such illumination as was granted to St. Ignatius could be a wonderful experience in the life of any man, but these insights can have real meaning only if we make ourselves channels of blessings.

Regardless of our state of grace, we must always seek His will and whatever we receive we must pass on to others. The Cayce readings seldom mention sudden insights as a key to successful living. They constantly emphasize the need for balance, discipline, and purpose, for "Understanding will come as quietly as the silent shadows of night, and His everlasting peace will live in our hearts." *(A Search for God)*

In all spiritual studies, there is a constant need to relate the spiritual to the physical and the mental. We speak of "Mind the Builder" and "Co-creators with God"; but how do these concepts make an individual a better stockbroker, housewife, or plumber? Will these lofty precepts help us to raise our children, become good citizens, or enlarge our circle of friends? Our lives can be made better in every way, according to the readings, if we constantly ask ourselves this question: What is my ideal? In other words, why do I want more friends? Why do I wish to become a better stockbroker? Do I wish to become a better housewife and raise my children well to satisfy my own selfish needs or do I want to do these things in order to glorify God by serving others? The tremendous significance of the Cayce readings lies in their relation to our daily activities.

Over and over again, they tell us, we can be successful in any line of work, whether it be lofty or menial, if our ideal is high. Everything we do can bring us closer to God.

We can apply the same discipline in daily activities that we do in meditation.

**In budgeting thy time, do not set thyself to activities spasmodically—for body improvement in *any* respect, or periodically; but rather systematically. Ye would learn, then, not to become a slave to custom. Ye do not become a slave to smiling, not to loving,**

**not to being a friend, not to thinking good. These become a part of thy whole being.**

**So in thy budgeting, let the activities be consistent and persistent; and so with the use of goods and stimulants to the body. Use when *needed* but don't overdo and do not become a slave to habit. 1206-13**

Here we are advised to use not only discipline but also moderation and not to let our daily activities become routine. Even the most menial task can become a source of infinite reward if it is done in the right spirit. If we constantly think of a higher purpose, then every step we take, day by day, will bring us closer to God.

Is it practical to strive for an ideal that is apparently unattainable? "To dream the impossible dream" is the only practical way to love; we are much better off as result of our struggle for perfection. The goal may be remote, but the thrust for its attainment brings new tests of strength, new challenges, and numerous opportunities to serve others. Even if we fall far short of our goal, we are better off than if we had never attempted the struggle.

**Then, the try may be counted to thee as righteousness . . . righteousness is of God. 3621-1**

Just as the aim of art is beauty, the aim of religion is the search for God. Art and religion are both at an end when we cease the search. Our ideal ceases to be our ideal once we have it in our grasp. *Seek . . . the kingdom of God, and his righteousness . . .* (Matt. 6:33) Jesus does not tell us when we will find it but merely that we are to seek!

Considering the complex problems of karma and reincarnation, we realize that prayer, meditation, and striving for the ideal bring the only solution to the problem of self-development. These efforts not only relate to our success on the earth plane but also help us to become "companions and co-creators with God" throughout eternity. What should be our ideal? Its selection and attainment are determined by sincerity of purpose and service to others.

In order to test our sincerity and purity of purpose we must constantly ask ourselves: Do I truly forgive? Am I in truth repentant? Am I a channel of love and mercy and grace? Is there room for improvement in my life? Do I need to change? More important, am I willing to change?

How do we test sincerity in others? Remember ... *with what measure ye mete, it shall be measured to you again.* (Matt. 7:2) In other words, you can't measure sincerity unless you are sincere yourself, for you apply the same test to others that you apply to yourself.

The ideal of service is mentioned in the New Testament time and time again. *Come unto me, all ye that labor and are heavy laden, and I will give* you *rest.* (Matt. 11:28) Most of us are inclined to avoid people who are in trouble and may become a burden to us. However, Jesus asked the heartsick, the weary and the burdened to come to Him. *Take my yoke upon you, and learn of me; for I am meek and lowly in heart: and ye shall find rest unto your souls.* (Matt. 11:29) Here is an unusual approach to successful living. Jesus is meek and mild, not arrogant, ambitious, or competitive. He asks you to take on a yoke in order to find rest for your soul. *For my yoke is easy, and my burden is light.* (Matt. 11:30) You may ask yourself: Who carries the lightest burdens in this life? It is those, and only those, who work to serve others. This lightened burden is found in the radiant love of a mother with a baby in her arms, in the quiet devotion of a priest in a leper colony. It is found in the enthusiasm of a teacher who watches a mentally retarded child form its first letter.

**Do not be afraid of giving self in service, if ... the *ideal* is correct. If it is selfish or for aggrandizement, or for obtaining a hold to be used in an underhanded manner—*beware*. If it is that the glory of truth may be made manifest, *spend it all*, whether self, mind, body, or worldly means—whether in labor or in the coin of the realm. 1957-1**

For until ye are willing to *lose* thyself in service, ye may not indeed know that peace which He has promised to give all. 1599-1

In thy service to those thou would entertain, keep ever in the attitude that something is given out that arouses hopefulness in the experience of the individual, group or the masses that ye would entertain. For whether ye preach a sermon or entertain—let it be done with an eye-singleness of joy, or helpfulness to thy fellow man . . . As ye give, as ye do unto thy fellow man, ye are doing unto the God in thyself. 877-3

For no matter what ye say, the manner in which ye treat thy fellow man is the answer to what ye really believe. The manner in which ye treat thy neighbor is the manner in which ye are treating thy Maker. 3684-1

Let your prayer continuously be: *Lord, use me, such as I am, in Thy kingdom.* And mean it, and *do it.* 3138-1

You'll not be in heaven if you're not leaning on the arm of someone you have helped. 3352-1

Each appearance in the earth is an opportunity given thee by the grace of God. 3003-1

Where you are—wherever you are! . . . the place whereon thou standest is holy ground. 2981-2

# The Bond of Being:
## Edgar Cayce on Love

### by Margaret Jett

FOR THE MESSAGE you heard from the very beginning is this: we must love one another. (1 John 3:11) Jesus talked a great deal about love, and so did Edgar Cayce. Two thousand years after the Christ showed us the power of love, we still need to be reminded of it again and again.

Love is a little word with sweeping multiple connotations. In the readings, Cayce spoke of love of country, love of beauty, love of fellow man, and, most important, the love that God shows for His children.

Monstrous mass media crying for money and attention have given love overblown sexual overtones. Many, inspired by Sigmund Freud, believe that man's primary unconscious goal is to realize uninhibited infantile sexuality. Mouthwash, toothpaste, and hair spray are now heavy artillery in the battle for desirability. Marriages continue to be entered into early, far too often to be dissolved bitterly.

The problem of the exploitation and ruination of love existed in the 1930s when Cayce gave the bulk of the readings. For centuries man has misunderstood and misused his creative love force. Now is the time for us to read and to heed our prophets. Surely, Edgar Cayce was such a man.

## The Meeting of Mates

Second only to "balance" the key word in the readings seems to be "purpose." The commonly held belief about meetings and circumstances is that they are pure chance, accident, or fate. Viewing our lives as purposeful and meaningful adds a new and important dimension.

**Hence in the relationships, the meetings with others in *whatever* form or manner, such are not coincidental but are rather as purposeful experiences. 1722-1**

If *every* meeting has purpose, how much more worthy of attention are those intimate friendships and loves which arise in each experience?

*(Q) Had I known my husband before?*

**(A) Known him several times before, some to good, some to bad. That's why those misunderstandings, and yet that which holds thee together! 1620-2**

Reincarnation in the Cayce philosophy becomes an explanation for present attractions and repulsions. Often those who were closely associated in past lives build loves.

*(Q) There is a man whom I met very recently and, upon our meeting, we knew right away that we had known each other before, and had been together before this incarnation. What were we to each other in the past and what will be our present relationship?*

**(A) The associations and relations in the experience just previous to this as well as in the Palestine**

**sojourns ... As to what these relationships will be in the present, it depends upon the application and the purposes—whether for the material or the mental or *spiritual* benefits. These should work to the better advantage of all. 1552-1**

## Loving and Being Loved

Each of us needs to receive and to express love. Even science has experimented in the field of love. Psychologists have found that babies fed and clothed adequately but deprived of human affection do not grow normally—physically or otherwise.

Cayce recognized and utilized astrological signs in aiding those who came to him. In the readings, Venus represents the state of consciousness an entity has experienced which may influence his love relationships.

**In that of Venus ... we find those of the fair sex are ever in the position of ruling much in the life. 520-1**

**From Venus we find abilities for great emotions as to conditions, experiences, friendships, loves in the material as well as the mental and spiritual. 1552-1**

Whether or not one knows of either his past lives or his astrological bent, he can benefit from the universal significance Cayce attached to the "like begets like" idea.

**Then, if you would have love, know that you must show yourself lovely. 1602-1**

This reading exemplifies the mutual give and take attitude so essential in approaching true harmony with another:

*(Q) (man, age 47) What should I do in connection with a recently begun friendship with a young girl?*

**(A)** *Friendship* **is beautiful. Do not make it possessive, for it becomes sin. 1827-1**

## Plato, Christ, and Cayce on Ideals

Along with purposeful meetings and loving friendships, Cayce emphasized the ideal reached for in human relationships. Plato introduced the concept of ideals into Western thought in 400 B.C. He believed in an unseen world from which this world drew for its meaning. All things that men call beautiful, for example, such as a small child, a rose, a poem, would each somehow be participating in the unseen ideal "Beauty." Cayce combined Plato's thought with the message of the Christ. In *A Search for God, Book I*, "What Is My Ideal?" we read: "The true ideal is the highest spiritual attainment to be reached on this material plane; hence, it follows that our ideal must be found in Christ, Who is the Way." For one person to make this ideal his own and work toward its fruition is a life's work. For two to work together in this becomes quite a task, a labor of love.

*(Q) Should I marry the girl to whom I am engaged?*

(A) As we find, if the ideals of each are compatible, it may be made to be an experience worthy of acceptance. 1861-2

*(Q) Do you find any particular individual with whom I would be happiest?*

(A) This should be the choice within self; for as individuals meet individuals there are those associations and contacts that bring out the best in each, or there may be those karmic influences to be worked out together . . . Choose one that is in accord, however, with some of the activities thou desirest to make as ideals—not as just ideas—in the experience. 520-3

. . . live thine own life, and use each associate, each opportunity, as the means for giving expression to that which *is* thy ideal. 1551-2

*(Q) (girl, age 15) Is the entity too active socially?*
(A) No; for the entity is well balanced in this respect: Just keep that ideal . . . Those associates in social affairs *must* measure to an *ideal* or the entity *cannot associate* with such. *Do not lower the standard.* 1738-1

## Marriage as the World's Hope

Commitment between a man and a woman is much more than a social contract or a convenient arrangement for legal sex relations. Many times the readings elevate marriage to the lofty position it merits.

What is thy ideal relationship as to home? For, know that such is as a pattern of that *hoped* for in a heavenly home. And if each entity would so live in this material sojourn as if it were for an eternal home, much more beauty, much more joy, much more peace would be attained. 1872-1

The readings admonished prospective partners:

There is rarely given the proper consideration to the union of individuals for the bringing of the young into the world. 1592-1

This optimistic note speaks to those willing to seek out and follow love ideals.

It need not be stressed as to the necessity or the importance of building a home, for as is understood—this is the source of hope for the world! 1891-1

## More Questions than Answers

Only a very few who had readings were directly advised on possible marriage matches.

And well that the body choose that one who has black eyes, brown hair, as a mate, not the gray with light hair. 553-1

*(Q) Would it be best for me to marry him if he agrees?*
(A) Never! 1754-1
Most young people were cautioned to take their time in making such a decision as that concerning life partnership. Cayce frequently suggested waiting until the twenty-seventh or twenty-eighth year for union.

Instead of being given instant advice, almost all were asked more questions; were asked to look within self.

*(Q) With which one of these [women] would marriage be successful?*

**(A) This should be determined by the entity itself, in the studying, analyzing of the purposes and ideals.**

**For in consideration of marriage—if it is to be a success—it must be considered not from merely the outward appearance, as physically; for these soon fade. Rather it should be considered from the angle of spiritual ideals, mental aspirations and physical agreements. These should be analyzed in the experience of the entity . . . 1776-2**

*(Q) Is Dr.—— the proper mate for the body?*

**(A) The body should decide for itself. Use its mind for some direction, at least! 1733-1**

With the advent of the Pill and shouts of free love from youth, the question of premarital sex has simultaneously become more liberated and more bound. The sex question is more liberated in the sense that Dr. Haim Ginott expresses in *Between Parent and Teenager:* "In the past a girl could use the fear of pregnancy as an excuse for chastity. Now this excuse is gone." There is still much that is bound despite this partial freedom. Parents cry out in objection, and youth continues self-conscious questioning about intimate relationships. This kind of biological freedom must not be the satisfactory answer. Cayce recognized the turmoil that questions of sex can bring.

**This is ever and will ever be a question, a problem
until there is the greater spiritual awakening within
man's experience, this phase biologically, sociologi-
cally ... must be as a stepping stone for the greater
awakening. 1557-4**

The Edenic parable in Genesis describes man's original
sin as putting self above God, disobedience to the Father's
will. According to Cayce, attention to sex and other animal pleasures first turned man from God. This very sin,
however, can be transformed and used for good.

**Train them [children] in the sacredness of that
which has come to them as a privilege, a heritage;
from a falling, to be sure, but through the purifying
of the body in thought, in act, in certainty it may
make for a people, a state, a nation that may indeed
herald the coming of the Lord. 1556-7**

*(Q) Is marriage as we have it necessary and ad-
visable?*

**(A) *It is!* 1556-7**

Cayce reminds us what Jesus said about union: "For He
hath given that in the heavenly state there is neither marriage nor giving in marriage for they are as One." (1577-6)
The reading realistically continues: " . . . yet ye say ye are
on the earth, ye are born with the urge!" This state of being "in" yet not "of" the world can be met by practicing the
highest ideals on earth.

*(Q) Should there be sex relations outside of mar-
riage?*

**(A) This again is a matter of principle within the
individual ... if it has chosen not to be in such relationships then be true to the choice or else it is to
self a sin. One which would pretend to be and isn't,
is indeed sin.**

It may be inferred from the readings that Cayce would
not advocate breaking either the laws of man or God; he
stressed God's laws as primary and eternal.

Those then that besmirch same [sex] by overindulgence besmirch that which is best within themselves. And that should be the key to birth control or sex relations or every phase of the relationship between the sons and daughters of God. 1576-6

## Helpmeets for Life

Sometimes marriage was not advised for two with similar goals.

*(Q) Can we work and do big things for humanity without being married together?*

(A) Without being married together in the present experience. 1554-6

Cayce's definition of "soul mate" can apply on many levels of human relationships. A soul mate is found "where they are a complement one to another—not that as from physical attraction but for mental and spiritual help." (1556-2)

Friends or lovers, business partners or fiancés all were given practical—yet spiritual advice.

*(Q) What are David's peculiarities and what are mine so that we may adjust our lives harmoniously?*

(A) These, as indicated, are to be studied in each other; and the peculiarities, the oddities, the errors are to be minimized, *not* dwelt upon and increased. Minimize rather than crystallize the faults in the other. *Know* that thy associations are to be on a fifty-fifty basis, not forty-sixty nor twenty-eighty but *fifty-fifty.* 1722-1

Let each be rather a helpmeet, and not as a drudge to the other! 1669-1

Keep in that way that each may not make life in the physical a burden to the other, giving of self in physical, in spiritual, in all forces for their union should be perfect in each other and in *Him.* 254-8

The only true freedom for a Christian is in bondage to God's will. Cayce expresses an analogue to this freedom in the terms of human love. Only this special kind of "free love" can liberate us to greater service.

**The individual entity must be *free!* Yet the associations will ever bring that *bond of being* bound by the greater good to be accomplished for mankind, as a whole. 1554-6**

# How to Be a Channel Through Music

## by Linda Lee Stryker

THE CAYCE READINGS tell us that music has a unique bridging or spanning quality which sets it apart from all other arts. Dozens of readings refer to this by saying, music is " . . . that alone which may bridge the distance from the material to the spiritual." (2280-1)

**Only music may span that space between the finite and the infinite. 2156-1**

**[Music] alone may span the distance between the sublime and the ridiculous, between spirit and body, mind and soul. 3253-2**

Whenever we have a gulf in our personal or psychological lives such as going from an interest in materiality to something better, or from pessimism to optimism, or from feeling forsaken to feeling redeemed—we need a bridge to get to that other side. The readings tell us that music can supply the bridge we need, and is a way for us to be a channel of blessings to others. This can be our highest calling:

**For as ye pour out self, in a way to be of help to others, ye are the greater help to thyself. 5253-1**

In order to be a channel of blessings the things a person thinks, says, and does must not be done for self-gain or for self-aggrandizement. The blessings of our Creator must be allowed to flow through us, without thought of our own egos, *to* all those with whom we come in contact to *serve selflessly.*

We all have our preferences in music and almost all groups have their identifying music. Our current generation gap consists, in part, of an aversion to each other's music. Although for the two groups to get together on music might be impossible, this is not to say that either is necessarily better than the other. Each can, and does, serve a purpose.

**. . . the fruits thereof are the tests of whether the sources of supply are of the Creative Forces or the degrading forces . . . 5752-3**

## Benefits of Music Study

The readings mention often that each soul ought to include music as a part of his development (e.g., 2780-3). This doesn't mean that everyone should become a musician but it does indicate that the study and use of the art is a healthy influence for all.

According to the Cayce material, music in any shape or form can be a very great contribution to the individual, to the family, and to the community. One reading says that we should all express ourselves musically in one way or another, even if it is simply singing and humming around the home. Another reference stated that *anyone* could sing who could speak, and that the ability is not necessarily a gift given only to some and not to others. It goes on to maintain that anyone who practices with the thought of improving can, with patience, train the voice for singing in the community chorus or church choir and contribute in this way. Even if the voice is not of high quality, a person who sings around the home—not *to* anyone, but just in doing the regular chores—can be helpful to the family and keep the one who sings or hums lovely and beautiful (cf. 578-2).

We can be of service to our families by encouraging music study, because the readings say that in this way we also learn history and mathematics.

**If you learn music, you'll learn most of all there is to learn—unless it's something bad. 3053-3**

The following reading seems more precise about what is meant by learning other subjects: " . . . make music!"

**For this, if it is practiced, will tend to create the ability to commune with, to outline for the entity, that which has been the greater unfolding experience through the sojourns in the earth, as well as through those environs or vibrations during the interims. 5201-1**

It seems clear that the study of music helps bring forward things which we have already learned in earlier lifetimes. One person was advised to study woodwind instruments because it would help him recall a life as a shepherd during the time of Jesus and all the attendant pleasant associations.

Music, then, besides being a bridge to *past experiences*, nurtures creativity and sensitivity to art and beauty. It helps in the unfolding of individuality and enhances spiritual growth.

The following suggestions were given for parents who want their children to benefit from lessons. First of all, music lessons should never be a hardship or a chore; they should be happy experiences. Second, should the lessons become burdensome, there might be a change to a different instrument or another of the arts (painting, dancing, writing, etc.). Third, music should be a means of expressing the emotions, emotions that perhaps could not be expressed in other ways. A fourth, very important suggestion is that rather than too much emphasis on rote in the music lessons, the focus should be the beauty of the music and its expression. The final suggestion is that the pupil must have a desire to learn or the lessons won't be worth much. This means that parents who force a child into music before he is ready or before he *wants* to take lessons are not necessarily being helpful. This, more than likely, can even instill a distaste or even a hatred for music.

For those of us who are beginning to study music the Cayce readings have encouragement. They advise that in our practicing we should see and hear in each note "a song, a note of praise raised to Him, who is the giver of all good and perfect gifts." (3053-3) This is really difficult because practice can be tedious, yet seeing in each note a song of praise and a song of thanksgiving is a way to make the tedium disappear.

In one reading the question was asked, "What should be my attitude of mind about trying to learn singing to progress most rapidly?" The answer was *not "study more"* or *"practice more."* It was " . . . deep *meditation* with the awareness that His presence is so nigh unto thee." (1158-10) This suggests that much of a person's musical ability and power comes from his mental attitude. Then, once the technical proficiency and the mental attitude are balanced, " . . . music and art must come from the soul, to be worth while." (3440-1)

A young musician who wondered about her success in music was told:

**First find self . . . In the study and the analysis of self, use as the pattern the life of the Master, in that**

**given in the Sermon on the Mount . . . Find in self the answers to all the doubts and fears. 3234-1**

Her secondary duty was to make music her life's work. In this way she would receive many opportunities for being a channel of blessings to others and for bringing peacefulness to herself.

**Study the music and apply same . . . for in that field ye will find harmony of life, harmony of expression, harmony of relationships to Creative Forces. 2323-1**

These are the benefits of music study.

## Music as a Healing Force

The concept of music as a healing force was a major revelation for me. All my life I wondered about the positive advantages of music and what I was contributing as a musician.

A few months ago, I came across this verse in Samuel:

*"And it came to pass, when the evil spirit from God was upon Saul, that David took an harp, and played with his hand: so Saul was refreshed, and was well, and the evil spirit departed from him."* I Samuel 16:23

According to this verse, music is an extremely powerful force and is certainly a valuable contribution. King David, the harpist, knew about the power of music as, no doubt, had others before his time. I wondered if this knowledge was innate in the emphasis on music in the synagogues and churches of today. I wondered if the great composers all through the ages had known of this healing power and had infused it into their music. Eventually it seemed to me that *everyone* knows this fact about the healing power of music.

These statements from the Cayce readings needn't surprise us:

**. . . the music that quiets, through the vibrations**

**that are set off by such. 694-2**

**When illness or the like were to come about, soft music and the lighter shades or tones will quiet where medicine would fail. 773-1**

**And whenever there are the periods of depression, of the feeling low or forsaken, play music; especially stringed instruments of every nature. These will enable the entity to span that gulf as between pessimism and optimism. 1804-1**

Here again a reference to the bridging and spanning quality of music. This time bridging to heal, to lift up from feeling low, to reclaim the forsaken, to make an optimist out of a pessimist. The healing powers of music were mentioned often in the readings, which said that not only is the body healed and comforted but so is the mind.

**There may be the vibrations by chords and characters of music in which there may be assistance brought not only to the mentally deficient, the mentally twisted, the mentally unbalanced, but to even those who have characters of natures of fevers . . . 949-12**

Therapy and rehabilitation in many mental institutions include not only arts and crafts but also the playing of and listening to music. One person was to entertain in hospitals and institutions:

**. . . as part of the entity's endeavor to reclaim individual entities that are disturbed by nerve or shell shock or long weariness in the out-of-the-way places. 3908-1**

Musical notes within our hearing range are usually between 15- to 20,000 cycles per second. But here again, music has a strange quality—the notes which we hear are the starting tones for a whole series of vibrations which rise upward, most out of hearing range. This series is called the "overtone series." All instruments and the human voice produce overtones, each in its own particular way, and this accounts for the differences in tone qualities. As the series rises, going up past our physical hearing range, it goes into the frequencies of light and color, even up to odors, x-rays, and cosmic rays. You have perhaps heard of psychics or other gifted people who claim to see colors when they hear music or who hear music when they view a sunset or a painting. This is possible. They are receiving the higher—unheard, but not unperceived—vibrations. These very high vibratory rates are what affect our minds and bodies in a way that produces healing. " . . . there is much music in the makeup of the body . . . " (4531-2) Perhaps the high vibrations in the overtone series cause an answering resonation in the parts of the body that respond to the certain rate of vibration. We must harmonize this outer music with the inner music.

The readings suggest ways to harmonize.

**Think, for a moment, of the music of the waves upon the shore, of the morning as it breaks with the music of nature, of the night as it falls with the hum of the insect, of all the kingdoms as they unite in their song of appreciation to an all-creative influence that gives nature consciousness or awareness of its being itself. And harmonize that in thine own appreciation . . . 2581-2**

**What greater joy may there be than in the attuning of the harmonies of nature, the harmonies of the love of the Father as expressed through music! 827-1**

Harmony seems to be the important clue in the type of music that heals. When Cayce occasionally prescribed melodies like the *Blue Danube* and the *Spring Song*, his selections were ones with very little dissonance, and quite mild dissonance at that. These songs stressed simple harmonies and basically a strong, uncomplicated overtone series. It is apparently better for the series to rise unimpeded by complexity in order for healing to take place.

**As to thy music, in this thy hands may bring the consciousness of the harmonies that are created by the vibrations in the activities of each soul; that each other soul may, too, take hope; may, too, be just kind, just gentle, just patient, just humble. 518-2**
Vibrations in the activities of the soul create harmonies, and music brings this into consciousness. *Music brings activities of the soul into consciousness.* And in so doing can help others to become kind, gentle, patient, and humble.

The ways to be channels with music as a healing force are many. We can comfort our family with music and if we *won't* play or sing or hum we can see to it that the record player or radio plays soft music. We can bring music into hospitals and institutions or at least we can support these programs. We can harmonize—with nature, with each other, and with the Father who loves us and heals us always.

**Embrace Him while ye may, in music . . . 5265-1**

# Expanding the Afternoon Years

by Worth Kidd

ONE OF THE fascinating things about the Edgar Cayce philosophy as expressed through the A.R.E. Study Groups is its agelessness. The universal laws which are worked with in the groups apply to young and old, rich or poor, intellectual or otherwise. No matter at what age one encounters Edgar Cayce on one's walk through the earth plane, the simple truths speak eloquently to all. Here is certainly one area where there is no generation gap, and this is borne out by the philosophy itself, according to which the really important parts of us—our eternal souls—were all created at the same time "in the beginning." At least soul-wise, we are all the same age.

When a young man accepts the concept of reincarnation, he realizes he is not an unwilling victim of circumstances who was born at the wrong time, in the wrong body, to parents not of his choosing. On the contrary, he accepts the logic of being here because of the needs of his soul for development; so he needed to be here at this time, with the very parents he himself chose, in the environment also of his choosing and in the sex best suited for developmental needs. Also he realizes that his destiny for tomorrow, for the balance of this earthly sojourn and on into eternity is shaped and modified by what he does from moment to moment. He is responsible for his destiny and knows he has no excuse for self-pity, for blaming his parents or the environment, his education or religion.

Prayer and meditation as emphasized in the A.R.E. groups is also ageless. The young man can strip aside his ego and enter into the silence when he accepts the disciplines of the group just as readily as the older man. The same guidance is available for all whether in prayer, meditation, or dreams. The young can just as easily learn to catch and interpret dreams and use them for spiritual guidance to supplement the response obtained in meditation. Prayer, meditation, and dreams are practical tools which have been proven over and over in the A.R.E. group experience.

In the middle years, the A.R.E. group can be equally effective in helping its members express love and service to others and receive many unexpected fringe benefits in increased sensitivity and keener awareness of the needs of others. Facility equal to that of the younger or older members is found in prayer, meditation, and dreams.

In the later years and particularly after retirement, there is no better time for A.R.E. group participation. These mature people can bring to the group a wealth of experience and a range of viewpoints which can enrich group discussions and provide depth to the disciplines. No one is too old to share experience, hope, love, and wisdom with others; to be of unselfish service to others.

Many facets of the Edgar Cayce philosophy are helpful to the elderly, but the continuity of life concept is most reassuring, pointing out as it does that there is an endless future to work out all the things we wished to have done in this lifetime. When the present flesh body is laid aside, we, as souls, move on into another dimension carrying with us the memories of our past experiences in many other sojourns.

There are many ways of extending existence today which are rewarding to the extent that the additional years are lived creatively and zestfully.

Mature retired persons still want to be loved, appreciated, and needed. It is important for them to be useful and helpful, to express themselves creatively. Maturity at any time, and particularly in the later years, seems to require us to give of whatever we can—a smile, a cheerful word, a willingness to share of oneself. Loving maturity includes concern and respect for others and a real effort to understand them and help them grow through love, gentleness, kindness, and good will. Maturity includes the ability to examine concepts which were formerly considered valid and to replace them where necessary with new facts. The "good new days" may be better than "the good old days."

High on the list of the requirements for maturity is one's concept of God and the concept of one's relationship to the Father. Questions such as: "How did I get here, and why? Have I been here before?"

"What was and is God's purpose with me?"

"What is my purpose . . . now and into eternity?"

"What will eternity be like?"

These and related questions are answered in diverse ways by various religions and philosophies. Many people have found that the philosophy of the Edgar Cayce readings as expressed through the A.R.E. Study Groups not only provides satisfactory answers to these questions but stimulates mature living. Group members become channels of blessings in love and service to others.

The philosophy of the readings includes the following concepts:

## There Is a God

**What is thy God? Are thy ambitions only set in whether ye shall eat tomorrow, or as to wherewithal ye shall be clothed? Ye of little faith, ye of little hope, that allow such to become the paramount issues in thine own consciousness! Know ye not that ye are His? For ye are of His making! He hath willed that ye shall not perish, but hath left it with thee as to whether ye become even aware of thy relationships with Him or not. In thine own house, in thine own body, there are the means for the approach through the desire first to know Him; putting that desire into activity by purging the body, the mind, of those things that ye know or even conceive of as being hindrances . . . He is not far from thee! He is closer than thy right hand. He standeth at the door of thy heart! Will ye bid Him enter or will ye turn away? 281-14**

## We Can Relate to God Through Prayer, Meditation, and Dreams

**He that would know the way must be oft in prayer, joyous prayer, knowing He giveth life to as many as seek in sincerity to be a channel of blessing to someone; for, "Inasmuch as ye did a kindness, a holy work . . . to one of these, the least of my little ones, ye have done it unto me!" 281-12**

**Through regular periods of meditation we grow in grace, in knowledge, in understanding. We do not put on righteousness at that time as a cloak which may**

be laid aside when we are through. Rather we gird ourselves with it as we become one with Him. Our speech, our manner of activity, our life shows forth what we have become. If you would be a channel of blessing . . . consecrate your time, dedicate a period to meditation every day. 281-60

*(Q) Will I be able to interpret those [dreams] that come through me?*

(A) If thou will only open self to be a channel. 262-35

## The Real, Eternal Part of Us Is the Soul

For the entity is body, mind and soul. The soul is eternal—it is individual. The mind is the builder . . . The body is merely the channel through which there is material activity. 2550-1

The evolution of the soul . . . took place before man's appearance . . . in the material world. 900-19

All the souls were made in the beginning. We have entered again and again for the experience of the soul and to become one with the Creative Forces . . . 364-24

## The Soul Enters the Earth Plane with a Purpose

For the experience or sojourn in the earth is not chance but is in the natural spiritual and soul evolution of each entity that it may grow aware of its relationship to God—through its relationships to its fellow men; recognizing in each soul . . . those possibilities, those opportunities, those duties, those obligations, that are a portion of each soul entity's manifesting in a material plane. 2271-1

. . . for this is the purpose for which a soul comes into manifestation in or out of materiality; that it

may be one with, in companionship with, the creative
forces we call God. 826-2

## The Purpose Is Affected by Former Lifetimes

. . . the entity is that combination of the physical
body throughout all its experiences in or through the
earth, in or through the universe, and the reactions
that have been builded by those various or varied
experiences . . . Then for the *entity* to create, or give,
or be life, it must be a living, acting example of that
it is, and not as something separated, inactive, inanimate, not giving but gradually deteriorating . . .
As soon as it becomes an inanimate object (though
it may be serving a purpose), it *immediately begins*
to deteriorate, disintegrate. *Be* an entity! Be a *living* entity! 262-10

## All Our Lifetimes Follow the Law of Reincarnation and Karma

Thus the pattern, the book of life, is written by
the entity by its use of truth, knowledge and wisdom
and by its dealings with its fellow man through the
material sojourns. Also during the interims between
the material sojourns, there is consciousness, or
awareness. For the soul is eternal; it lives on; it has
a consciousness and awareness of that which it has
builded. 2620-2

## Love Fulfills That Law

(Q) *What is the law of love?*
(A) Giving. As is given in this injunction, "Love
Thy Neighbor as Thyself." As is given in the injunc-
tion, "Love the Lord Thy God with all Thine Heart,

Thine Soul and Thine Body" . . . The gift, the giving,
with hope of reward or pay is direct opposition to
the law of love. 3744-5
Love is law. Love is giving. Giving is as God, the
Maker. 3744-2
Purposes and ideals are achieved through love and
service. 900-340

## Man's Will Creates His Destiny

In entering the earth's plane, either in the present
experience or others—let it be understood that the
will's force plays the greater part in the development
or retarding of an entity through the earth's experience . . . 5718-2
For you are indeed a god in the making, and He
would have you as one with Him. Yet the choices must
be made by you—else you become only an automa-
ton, capable of doing only that to which you have
been set as unchangeable. For though the law of the
Lord is ever the same, the ability to show forth the
law is according to individual application. 1440-1
No experience, no urge, no environ, may be
greater than the will of an entity. 954-1
*(Q) Is it proper to study planetary effects to bet-
ter understand our tendencies and inclinations?*
(A) When studied aright, yes. But the *will* is the
guiding factor. 3744-4

## Man's Mind Has Formative Power

Mind is the builder and that which we think upon
may become crimes or miracles. For thoughts are
things and as their currents run through the environs of an entity's experience these become barriers
or stepping-stones, dependent upon the manner in

which these are laid, as it were. For as the mental dwells upon these thoughts, so does it give strength, power to things that do not appear. And thus does indeed there become that as is so oft given, that faith is the evidence of things not seen. 906-3

For the entity is body, mind and soul. The soul is eternal—it is individual. The mind is the builder and weaves that into the being of the soul that it, the soul entity, presents to its Creator as the usage of the talents given. The body is merely the channel through which there is material activity. 2550-1

That our mind dwells upon, that our mind feeds upon, that do we supply to our body, yes, to our soul. 1567-1

## Man's Answer Lies Within Self

As given, in patience possess ye thy presence before the Throne. Seek oft, then, to gain an audience with thine inner self which bears witness before that Throne. With patience may this be reached; for as one loses their hold on self in the lack of patience, so does that give the opportunity for the entering in of those things that would make afraid. Not that one should remain unactive, or inactive, but in patience run the race that is set before thee, looking to Him, the Author, the Giver of light, truth and immortality. That should be the central theme in every individual. Not in submissiveness alone, but in righteous wrath serve ye the living God. 262-24

For, know (not as preaching), all of the good, all of God, all of bad, all of evil that ye may know is within thine own self. Thus it depends upon what spirit, what purpose, what hope ye entertain as to whether that ye desire to accomplish in thy experience is to be accomplished or not. 5332-1

Know that within self ye are an individual entity, a universe within self, with all the potential powers and faculties of the divine as well as the hellish! 5332-1

## Oneness

God seeks all to be one with Him. Since all things were made by Him, that which is the Creative Influence in every herb, every mineral, every vegetable, every individual activity, is the same force you call God, seeking expression! God said: "'Let there be light,' and there was light." This, you see, is law, this is love. 294-202

. . . Ye are a part and parcel of a Universal Consciousness, or God—and thus of all that is within the universal consciousness or the universal awareness, as the stars, the planets, the sun, the moon. Do ye rule them or they rule thee? They were made for thine own use, as an individual. Yea, that is the thought which thy Maker, thy Father—God thinks of thee. 2794-3

The Lord thy God is one. The self—as an individual entity, body, mind and soul—is one. The soul is a child of God, or a thought, a corpuscle in the heart of God. Yet the entity, thine own soul, has been given a will to use the attributes of soul, mind and body to thine own purposes. Thus as the individual entity applies self in relationship to those factors, the entity shows itself to be a true child, or a wayward child, or a rebellious child, of the Creative Force, or God.

The will, then, to do, to be one with that Creative Force, and thus fulfill the purposes for which the entity entered this present sojourn, is an evidence of the conditions just stated, if one accepts the fact that God is and that the ego, the thought of self is

His offspring. This is the accepting of the fact that ye always were, ye always will be, dependent upon the relationship or upon that ye do with thy will. 3376-2
Each entity is a part of the universal whole. All knowledge, all understanding that has been a part of the entity's consciousness, then, is a part of the entity's experience. Thus the unfoldment in the present is merely becoming aware of that experience through which the entity either in body or in mind, has passed in consciousness. 2823-1
For the entity, as each soul, is a portion of the whole. Thus, though a soul may be as but a speck upon the earth's environs, and the earth in turn much less than a mote in the universe, if the spirit of man is so attuned to the infinite, the music of harmony becomes as the divine love that makes for the awareness in the experience of the Creative Forces working with self for the knowledge of the associations with same. 1469-1

Other A.R.E. group discussion topics may include:
Attitudes and their effect on health
Health and healing prayer; diet, exercise, relaxation, eliminations
Ideals
Self-knowledge
Universal laws
Emotions
Balanced living
Rejuvenation and longevity
Vibrations
Glands
Psychic development
Astrological influences
Destiny

These concepts are discussed usually only as needed to assist the understanding and application of the material contained in the two books of *A Search for God.* For example, *A Search for God, Book 1,* starts with a chapter on Meditation and then follows with chapters on:

"Cooperation"—with the group, self, soul, family, culture, God.

"Know Thyself"—which points out our inherent grandeur, the barriers which prevent us from knowing ourselves, how to overcome these barriers and achieve our potentials.

"What Is My Ideal?"—how to establish ideals, goals, purposes, standards and live them with group help.

"Faith"—development of the inner knowledge of the Creative Forces which help us live our ideals.

"Virtue and Understanding"—living our ideals; understanding and using knowledge, moving in the right direction.

"Fellowship"—with our brothers and with God.

"Patience"—as an active, growing force in purposeful relationship with all of God's creations.

"The Open Door"—opening ourselves to God; becoming unselfish channels of love and service.

"In His Presence"—keeping the door open; "use me."

"The Cross and the Crown"—our attitudes determine which it shall be.

"The Lord Thy God Is One"—in oneness, attunement, at-onement.

"Love"—as God's expression through us.

The Edgar Cayce material does not attempt to foster any particular religion. It does enrich and extend spiritual understanding so that our own religion becomes more meaningful. It offers a contemporary and mature view of the reality of extrasensory perception, the importance of dreams, the logic of the continuity of life, the practical use of prayer and meditation in daily life, and a better understanding of the Bible.

Above all, the Cayce material is reassuring. It sets out good reasons for our presence in the earth plane and equally good reasons for moving on into other dimensions of eternal life. With group help, the material can quicken our awareness of our spiritual natures and help us *apply* this awareness in our daily lives so that we can live in a working relationship with the God within ourselves, the God in other people, and the God "out there." This means *living* the love of God, not only toward God, but for all His creations.

The A.R.E. Study Groups do not advance any dogma or creed. The group moderators advance challenging questions and keep the discussions channeled profitably, but each group member weighs and evaluates the information discussed and formulates his independent conclusions. He finds by experiencing and testing the values presented whether or not they are valid for him.

The groups are characterized by an atmosphere of tolerance, friendly interest, and acceptance. In this environment, there is an inducement for unusual freedom of expression which increases as members of the group learn to trust each other. As the group works together, the members not only find a new quality of association within the group but with all other people. Members find it easier to look at themselves, discover the roles they have been playing and the possible need to discard roles and false faces so they can find the freedom of being themselves.

Many who were groping blindly for a sense of right direction have found themselves in an A.R.E. Study Group where practical suggestions are tested and used among those who are developing tenderness, gentleness, kindness, forgiveness, patience, love, and self-knowledge. The attitude of each member is important in helping shape these values in oneself and by example, encouraging others to do likewise.

The A.R.E. group is not the only path to spiritual growth.

Any group that encourages the use of prayer and meditation and then requires that enlightenment be lived in line with the age-old teachings of Jesus is heading in the right direction. However, for many people, the Edgar Cayce material as developed through the A.R.E. groups, has provided answers they were unable to find elsewhere. These groups say to all: "Come and join with us."

# Psychic Phenomena and the Bible

by George Lamsa, Ph.D.

A FEW DECADES ago very few Christians in America and Europe realized that forty percent of the Holy Bible came through psychic perception; that is, in dreams, visions, and revelations which men of God saw when they meditated upon problems which their conscious minds could not solve.

Both in this country and abroad, the subject of psychic phenomena, dreams, and visions was largely ignored; notwithstanding that a large portion of the Scriptures came through such revelations. Jeanne d'Arc was burned at the stake because she said that she was called in a vision to help France at a critical time. In New England, men and women who claimed they had familiar spirits were persecuted or put to death.

All Hebrew prophets and seers were endowed with the gift of prophecy. Through their spiritual eyes they could see that which their physical eyes could not discern. Through their mystic sense they were enabled to transcend the material and physical world and eliminate time and space, and to see the rise and fall of great Empires which had not yet come into existence. In the realm of the Spirit, time and space do not exist and events which are to take place hundreds of years hence have already taken place. Nearly all of the predictions which have been made by the prophets have come true. Not one word has failed. Babylon and Ninevah are still in ruins and their sites are used by shepherds for encamping and grazing, just as was predicted centuries before Christ.

Psychic ability may be called the sixth sense; one which can foretell disasters, tragedies, and famines, and can also reveal periods of prosperity and happiness. The Hebrew patriarchs relied on guidance from visions and dreams for the welfare of their tribes. Pharaoh, who dreamed of seven lean and seven fat cows, and also seven full ears of wheat and seven blasted ones, was told of seven prosperous years which were to be followed by seven years of famine. No Egyptian was able to understand the symbolic language of Pharaoh's mysterious vision; only Joseph, the son of the last Hebrew patriarch, was able to interpret it because he had been trained by his father, Jacob.

Seemingly, the whole of nature is endowed with the sixth sense. Birds, animals, and fish have this sense in order that they may be guided in their migrations and to avoid danger.

When man discovered modern means of communications and transportation, he discarded the sixth sense and began to rely on his own wisdom and knowledge. When a sense is not used, sooner or later it becomes dormant. If we were to cover our eyes for several weeks, we would find it difficult to see with them. Or, if we were to tie one of our arms behind us for a month, it would become almost useless.

There is also the seventh sense, that is, man's knowledge of good and evil from which we have the concept of the Golden Rule; not to do unto others what you do not want them to do to you; and also the concept of the law of compensation, man reaps that which he has sown and gathers that which he has scattered. These laws are immutable, just as the rising and setting of the sun. All great nations that have taken the sword have perished by the sword. All those who have oppressed weaker nations have been oppressed. Assuredly, all men are endowed with seven senses which, whether they are used or not, are inherent in all generations.

Some of the Hebrew prophets were especially gifted psychically. In their dreams and visions they could converse directly with God. Others relied on symbols and similitudes which they saw in their dreams. Moses communed with God as one person communes with another.

The prophets acted as counselors for kings and princes. Although they were able to commune with God at any time, it was usually only during the night when nature is silent, for then the voice of God can be heard aloud.

Job says, "For God speaks once; he does not speak a second time; In a dream, in a vision of the night, when deep sleep falls upon men while slumbering upon the bed; Then he opens the ears of men and humbles them according to their rebelliousness." (Job 33:14-16)

This is why some of the prophets retired into the solitude of the deserts and desolate places where nature is still and where the voice of the Spirit is loud and the glory of God manifested. Here they fasted and prayed so that they might hear the inner voice, the voice of their Creator.

Even Jesus, with all of His knowledge of God and spiritual forces, had to retire into the desert to fast and pray so that He could be able to see the course of events which lay ahead of Him. This enabled Him to make the decision to embark on his great and hazardous mission. It was during these silent hours in the arid wasteland when He saw His triumph over evil forces and the road which would lead Him to the cross and His triumph over death.

Some of the prophets abstained from meat, wine, and strong drink, as did Daniel in order to be able to commune with spiritual forces. Consequently, they were able to transcend the material world and see the course of forthcoming nations, events which would take place centuries after their deaths.

The ability to prophesy was acquired through constant intensive study and meditation. During the time of Samuel there were schools wherein men were taught the rudimentary elements of prophesying.

The prophets played an important part in the history of religion. They shaped the destinies of great nations. In their dreams and visions they saw what the leaders of the world could not see.

Clues to their origin are clearly seen in the first verse of some of the books of the prophets. For example: The book of Isaiah begins with these words: "This is the vision of Isaiah which he saw during the days of certain kings." The book of Ezekiel in a similar way states, "This is the vision of Ezekiel." Other keynotes to indicate that Scriptures were received in a vision are these: *God appeared; I was in Spirit; the Spirit of the Lord came upon me; I was in a vision and I dreamt.* All of the books of the prophets came through high revelation and the authors were admonished by God to write messages in plain language so that the people could understand then.

Edgar Cayce stressed the importance of visions and dreams as a way to commune with spiritual forces. His telepathic-clairvoyant readings exemplified his ability to see both the past and the future, which in Spirit are one.

Today, we thank God that thousands of people are interested in the many areas of psychic investigation. These people see the great importance which the prophets of Israel played in changing the history of religion and the course of mankind.

What a blessing it will be to the world when this spiritual or mystic sense is recovered and once again put into use! Perhaps some day psychically gifted men of God will be consulted by the governments of the world just as the prophets and seers in the olden days were consulted by Kings and Emperors. Then religion will be a blessing to mankind.

# Journey in Consciousness

## by Robert F. O'Donnell

### Prologue

*. . . AND YOU SHALL know the truth, and the truth shall make you free.* John 8:32

The lamp was hung out in the Old North Church, Revere and Dawes began their midnight rides, and on the nineteenth of April, 1775, the battle for freedom began. The price was paid; freedom from tyranny was won; and the nation began. On the nineteenth of April, 1971, the author discovered the price for another kind of freedom . . . the freedom that comes with knowledge of the truth. This is the story of the events that led to that freedom and, perhaps more significantly, to the awareness of the price that must be paid.

*George and I were on an airplane, returning from a visit to Virginia Beach and the Association for Research and Enlightenment, when a brief encounter with a troubled stranger provided the back-drop against which the whole question of consciousness came into focus. It was a short flight, giving me just an hour in which to reexamine my own experience, one hour in which I hoped to find the right thing to say.*

*Ten years ago I had been torn apart by the same struggle with rituals and doctrines now confronting our fellow passenger. How had I survived the anger and violence of my own crisis of faith? What were the principles involved? If I could just pick up and follow the thread of my own growth in consciousness, perhaps I could find the words with which to help him.*

**Then a soul, the offspring of a Creator, entering into a consciousness that becomes a manifestation in any plane or sphere of activity . . . 5753-1**

Man, physical man and mental man, is a manifestation of consciousness. He *has* physical and mental (or human) consciousness which makes him aware of the sensate world about him, but in the spiritual sense he does not *have* consciousness—he *is* consciousness. Man, the real man, exists as a state of consciousness that is presently appearing in the earth as a flesh and blood body.

*This took some getting used to. I had always thought that I was real, you know. Now, let's see; I can see and feel myself—that's physical consciousness. And I can think of what I'm doing, have done, and will do—that's mental consciousness. Put them together and that's what you call human consciousness. Put them together with my body and you have what I used to call me, but which I now know as the appearance of me. This solved a lot of questions, especially ultimate ones such as the continuity of life.*

The Cayce readings show that this same principle holds

true for "any plane or sphere of activity." Thus it is not surprising to hear that:

**Death in the material plane is passing through the outer door into a consciousness in the material activities that partakes of what the entity, or soul, has done with its spiritual truth in its manifestation in the [earth] sphere. 5749-3**

Man enters the after-death state as another manifestation of the spiritual consciousness that he is. The human consciousness, man's interface with the physical world, gives way to a new type of consciousness, a consciousness having attributes suitable to the form man takes in what has been variously termed the astral, or spiritual plane.

Whatever that form might take, it is evident in the Cayce material that it too is only an appearance, another projection of spiritual consciousness into another plane of "material activities." Like the human body, the astral, spiritual, or soul body is not really man, but man appearing as the form and substance of that plane of awareness.

The nature of the soul body is given in the following readings:

**What one thinks continually, he becomes . . . After death the soul and spirit feed upon and, in a sense, are possessed by that which was created by the mind in the earth experience. Whatever has been gained in the physical plane must be used. 3744-4**

**What form, then, do such bodies assume? The _desired_ form!—built and made by that individual in its experience in the material plane. 5756-4**

Regardless of the plane on which our consciousness manifests itself, of this we can be sure: that the nature of that manifestation is a function of what we do about what we know. Whether we are moving into a physical existence to begin a new earth experience, or out of physical life into the spiritual plane, the transit of consciousness is nothing more nor less than a moving from the time of planting to the time of harvest. Here is no jumping out of a physical body into some vague state of eternal bliss or misery, but a meeting of self to reap what we have sown.

*My own struggle began with this question of life after death. I found it impossible to resolve the idea of an all-loving deity with eternal punishment for temporal failings. If I, as a very human father, couldn't even begin to entertain the idea of punishing the misdeeds of my children with a lifetime of suffering, how could I believe in a God who would be infinitely unforgiving? Because I couldn't believe it, it became increasingly more difficult to maintain confidence in the church that said I had to. The crisis had begun.*

## Limits of Consciousness

*"No man can reveal to you aught but that which already lies half asleep in the dawning of your knowledge."—Gibran*

What are the limits of awareness to which we may attain?

**For know, all that the entity may know of God, or even of law or international relationships *already exists in the consciousness* for the entity to be made aware of same. 4099-1**

**What, then, is the purpose of the entity's activity in the consciousness of mind, matter, spirit, in the present? That it—the entity—may know itself to *be* itself and part of the Whole, (not the Whole, but one *with* the Whole) . . . 826-11**

More specifically, the Cayce material tells us that the outer limit of consciousness, the Ideal, the goal of man, is the attainment of what the readings refer to as the Christ Consciousness:

*(Q) Should the Christ Consciousness be de-*

*scribed as the awareness within each soul im-*
*printed in pattern on the mind and waiting to be*
*awakened by the will, of the soul's oneness with*
*God?*

(A) **Correct. That's the idea exactly. 5749-14**

Man's purpose is to know himself to be himself, yet one with God. Not *become* one with God, but *become aware* that he is already one with Him. All that the Father has is already ours, residing in our spiritual consciousness awaiting its unfoldment. All the knowledge, all the health, all the wisdom, all the goods of the world are the Father's and it is the Father's good pleasure to give us the kingdom.

What is it then that hinders us? What is it that keeps us from realization of this great truth? Could it be that we have been looking for it across the sea or upon the mountaintop? Have we been looking for it in a book, a church, a creed, a teacher? If so, we have been looking in vain because all that the Father has "already exists in the consciousness for (us) to be made aware of it." All these sources may provide guidance, but the realization can only be found within. God is not withholding anything from us—He has placed it in our hearts that we might find it. It remains for us to open ourselves to receive it by acknowledging the presence of Christ in our own consciousness.

What is it that hinders us? We hinder ourselves. It is only by our action in the light of what truth is known to us that we become free to move to higher and higher levels of consciousness, greater and greater realization of our oneness with the Father. The elevation of consciousness is really the elevation of self with respect to the standard of divine truth, an ongoing, outpouring expression of the allness of God, revealing Himself as your consciousness and mine.

*You can imagine how confused I was at this point. If the Word of God was in my consciousness, I certainly didn't realize it. What puzzled me most was how, if this heritage was really mine, had I managed to become so separated from it?*

## The Separation

All of which leads to the question of why there is a separation between knowing the truth and being one with the truth. The Cayce readings show that man was created as a spiritual being, conscious of itself and of its oneness with the Father. This is the primal state and the ultimate goal of individual being. Individual spirit was consciousness without form or substance, in full awareness that its being and its power were God's being and God's power.

With free will, there was ever the possibility that individual consciousness could choose to act in defiance of that which it knew itself to be. When that first thought came of self as being apart from God, as having power of its own, the creative power of individual mind brought into being that which was imaged—a sense of separation.

Thus began the journey of the prodigal from his father's house. With each subsequent thought of self as a thing apart, the soul became less and less conscious of its oneness with its source and more and more conscious of itself as a thing apart. The separation was never real and is not real now, but so long as man persists in the illusion of separation he can never turn and begin the journey in consciousness back to his Father's house, back to conscious union with his Source. Only when we realize that this sense of separation is an illusion do we begin to know the truth that makes men free. Then, when the first faint light of this realization disturbs our sense of separate selfhood, the consciousness of separation takes on new meaning.

**What, then, is the meaning of the separation? [To bring] into being the various phases so that the soul may find in manifested forms the consciousness and**

**awareness of its separation, and [a return to] itself, by that through which it passes in all the various spheres [stages] of awareness. 262-56**

The distinction is subtle, but it is important to recognize the difference between thinking that we are separated from our Source and knowing that we have a *consciousness* of separation. In one case we are living under and are subject to all the drawbacks of an illusion; in the other case we may, if we choose, make a conscious effort to place our feet upon the spiritual path of return.

From the center of our being our individual will would awaken us to the knowledge of what we are, to the realization of our Christ Consciousness that is "imprinted in pattern on the mind." But will is under direction of the conscious mind, which has no desire to yield up its sense of separate selfhood.

**Mind is the factor that is in direct opposition to the will. 3744-1**

Is it any wonder that enlightened teachers throughout history have epitomized mind as the "slayer of the real"? It was the activity of mind that created and continues to maintain the great illusion, the false sense of separate existence, and it is through the activity of mind that the illusion must eventually be dispelled. But it must be through the *right activity* of mind. Too long has man allowed himself to be ruled by the musings of the mind when he should have been the master, using mind not as a container to be filled but as an avenue of awareness to the truth that is already within us.

*My human mind, in the early struggle between its ideas of God and those of the church, said, "If there is a God, will someone please demonstrate the fact!" And so it was that in my crisis of faith I moved from one concept to another, never realizing that all concepts formed in the duality of the human mind serve only to enhance our sense of separation, and keep us from the truth.*

Consciousness, then, is self in the process of becoming aware of itself as it unfolds toward its omega point through a gradual overcoming of the illusion of separation. That unfoldment can, according to the Cayce material, be completed in this life experience. Knowing this, we can move on to examine the principles governing the expansion of consciousness.

## The Expansion of Consciousness

The same laws governing the movement of consciousness from one plane to another apply equally well to the expansion of consciousness in the earth plane.

**This is shown to man in the elemental world about him . . . Hence as man passes through this material world, there are manifestations of the attributes that the consciousness finds coinciding with that activity which is manifested; hence becomes then as the very principle that would govern an entrance into further manifestations . . .**

**. . . every form of life that man sees in a material world is an essence or manifestation of the creator . . . 5753-1**

Since any manifestation in the earth is in essence an expression of God, we may, through observation, determine the principles which enable or bring about an elevation of consciousness. What are the principles which enable a tiny seed to grow into "further manifestations" as a stalk, a bud, a full-fledged flower? As we observe the flower we see the "attributes" of unending patience, the absence of thought for self, confidence, and reliance on nature for substance. The flower does not think it is a flower or that it is beautiful; it simply is. We see these attributes and we see that they "coincide with the activity" of the flower, the activity of growth toward fulfillment.

You might well ask, "What has this to do with man?" It is

simply that man, too, is a manifestation of God, one whose purpose also is to grow toward fulfillment. Although the fulfillment is different, the same principles which enable the simplest seed to reach its goal also enable man to evolve into higher and higher states of consciousness.

However, more than observation is required:

**Man's consciousness of that about him is gained through that [which] he, man, does about knowledge of that [which] he is, in relation to that from which he came and towards which he is going.** 5753-I

The Cayce readings emphasize that the unfoldment of consciousness toward conscious union with the Father is not a matter of the truth you know, but of what you *do* about the truth you know. The principles learned by observing the flower in its growth are of little value to us until we apply those principles in our own experience. It is only in the *application* of our knowledge of truth that we move to higher levels of awareness. In fact, the very perception of some of the principles governing growth is in itself the manifestation of a state of consciousness reached as a result of some prior application of knowledge held.

*It has been a long journey since the throes of dissent reduced my faith to the vanishing point and restructured my consciousness into that of a Christian Agnostic. Without any awareness of the principles involved, the action of my dissent had moved me from the herd consciousness of blind belief and unquestioning acceptance into a new consciousness of self as an individual, a thing apart and free. But I only thought I was free; I had arrived in a brilliant manner at a wrong conclusion.*

*Freedom? Oh, I was free of herd consciousness, but my freedom became the chains of a new imprisonment because I had simply exchanged the confinement of one set of human concepts for the confinement of another. In considering myself not just as an individual, but as an*

*individual apart from others, I proceeded to manifest
the nature of my new-found consciousness by criticiz-
ing every institution, practice, and ritual of my former
state whenever I had the chance.*

*There were chances aplenty. Everyone who still af-
firmed what I had rejected was a prime candidate for
attack . . . All of them, family, friends, acquaintances,
and even occasional strangers received a full barrage.
Was I good at it? You bet I was. I was so good at tying
people in mental knots that after three years of practice,
acquaintances were strangers, friends were acquaintances, and family—well, you know how families are.*

*And it was very, very lonely.*

## States of Consciousness

How many states of consciousness are there? We might
as well try to number the sands. Each state is different
because it is arrived at as a result of individual experience
and cannot be duplicated. Each state exists as a greater or
lesser sense of separation, with its attractions as well as
its dangers.

*When I discovered the phenomenon of Edgar Cayce
and the philosophy that came through him, my isolation
was complete. Those who didn't see me as an anti-reli-
gious iconoclast (partly true at the time) viewed me as
an occult kook (also partly true at the time), and there
just wasn't anyone with whom to share this new light.*

*One evening as I brooded over my fate, my wife, Pat,
called my attention to something I had overlooked in the
A.R.E. News. There it was, under "Groups in New Areas"—Whitman, Massachusetts, the very next town! I
believe I set a record in getting to the telephone that night.*

*Several evenings later I attended my first Study Group
meeting, and it seemed like a homecoming. The consciousness of oneness with these wonderful people swept*

*over and engulfed me and I haven't been the same since.
Meeting people who shared my beliefs ended my loneli-
ness. It was the beginning of a new life of spiritual
search and the prelude to my introduction to the real
spiritual problem of modern man.*

The attractions of any state are also dangers in that they
tend to keep man confined to that state. Each step in the
direction of expanded consciousness triggers opposing
forces within the human mind, forces that must be brought
into balance before we can move toward each succeeding
step. The closer we approach a new level of awareness
the stronger becomes the desire to dwell in its light, yet
the longer we dwell in any state of consciousness, the
more blinded we become to the light that lies beyond it.

It is in coming to this realization that:

**. . . man reaches the consciousness in the material
plane of being aware of what he does about or with
knowledge, intelligence, produces that which is
known as the entering into the first cause, principle,
basis or essence, that there may be demonstrated in
that manifested that which gains for the soul, for the
entity, that which would make the soul an acceptable companion to the Creative Force, Creative Influence. 5753-1**

Thus we learn that states of consciousness are not to be
sought for their own sake, but to be *passed through* on the
journey to the Father's house. We must be constantly alert
to the attractions of any state which would hinder us in
our unfoldment, not because there is any power for good
or evil in them, but because in the duality of our human
mind they can easily reinforce our sense of separate
selfhood.

*Although I didn't recognize it as a problem at the time,
many in our group had psychic experiences to relate,
and as time passed I became more and more fascinated
with phenomena. I found myself seeking psychic power*

*in the name of spiritual development.*

*It was a real spiritual problem because fascination with the psychic turns easily into dependence. Like Saul, I found myself seeking advice and guidance from the spirit world when I should have been turning to the Christ within. I saw that psychic ability could be sought, developed, and used for its own sake, and was blinded to the promise that all of this and more would appear as "added things" to those who seek first the Kingdom of Heaven within their own consciousness.*

Only by keeping our eyes fixed on the Infinite can we avoid the entrapments of the finite; only by acting in accordance with the truth we know is our consciousness lifted up; only by lifting up the consciousness of Christ do we find the truth that makes us free—free to walk unerringly the spiritual path to our Father's house.

## Epilogue

*I suppose it was meant to happen this way: the sand of Virginia Beach was still in my shoes, my spirit was riding high from the uplifting vibrations of a weekend of spiritual fellowship, when, fifteen thousand feet in the air, a passing stranger brought me face to face with the ghost of my former self.*

*I asked myself if it would do any good to repeat my own story, to tell him that I too had passed through the same crisis of faith that was tearing him apart. He said that he could find God as much in his garden as in his church, yet he didn't realize that what he said is the truth that could set him free. He didn't realize it and I didn't know how to tell him.*

*George didn't know either. I saw the anguish on his face; he too realized that this gap in consciousness could not be bridged by words. I had always thought that helping someone was an easy matter when you had had simi-*

*lar experiences yourself! Should I have told this stranger that he was moving through a stage of development and not to worry? Or should I have shared my experience and told him that my own faith was restored because of a man named Cayce who talked in his sleep?*

The unfoldment of spiritual consciousness is a journey that can only be made alone. This does not mean that we must turn our back on human love, concern, or fellowship, but that we must be prepared to give up our attachments to them and our desire to possess them. These are but the mirrors of the totality of Divine Love within each individual, and it is given us to seek their Source—not the reflected images.

When we have at last determined to put aside our desires and attachments, our sense of separation will begin to fade into a greater realization of our true relationship with all of creation.

# Karma and Grace: Jesus the Pattern

◆

## by Mark Martin Vieweg

DISCUSSIONS OF KARMA and grace in the Edgar Cayce readings present three basic concepts:

(1) The universe is governed by perfect unchangeable law (the essential law of like for like).

(2) It is man's birthright—the gift of free will—which governs his relationship to universal law through individual choices made.

(3) Man is always in some relationship to the law. He is either in karma or in grace. He does not escape it!

The key concepts then are law, free will, and a freely chosen relationship to the law. These three are unavoidable, undeniable, and eternal parts of creation, of man's co-creation with God.

The law is the law of like for like; we reap what we sow;

that which we choose creates the pattern, the mirror of that which must be experienced in our individual lives.

Free will is the power of a self-knowing, self-conscious entity to recognize alternatives within self, to freely choose a place in the law; to direct the patterns of like for like through self—through use of mind the builder.

The chosen relationship is always in either of two categories: (1) the individual under the law, which is karma; (2) the individual one with the law and above the law, which is grace.

To be in karma, to be experiencing karmic patterns from past choices, is to be living the letter of the law, or, at other times, to be rebelling against the law. It is misuse and misinterpretation of the law—using free will with selfish and unconstructive motives.

To be in grace is to use free will rightly in applying the principle of like for like with the spirit of truth and love in the full spirit of the law. Grace is man's knowing and living free use of law with constructive creative motives, purposed in others, not in self.

The Edgar Cayce readings show clearly how man individually chooses to abide either in karma or in grace as he strives to discover his personal relationship to God, to the law, and to the Creative Forces of the universe.

**For the experience of every soul in the material plane is not mere chance, but the fulfilling of that as was set in motion from the entrance of spirit into matter, that man may know his true relationship to the Creative Forces. 1786-1**

**. . . and for what purpose does an entity enter a material plane other than to prepare self for a better relationship to that for which it was in the beginning created, to be a companion with the Creator. 3579-1**

Man experiences life in the physical earth plane and in other levels of consciousness in order to discover his true relationship to God through individual application of the will.

. . . **what one does with one's experience, knowledge, or understanding makes for that which is the advancement or the retardment. For each soul must meet *itself* and its activity *in the earth* . . . For Life is One! And what ye sow, ye must also reap. 845-1**

**Each entity must answer for its own choosing . . . 1100-31**

**For the will is the gift of the Creator, enabling a soul to be one with God or—in its own wisdom or own foolishness—to destroy its own self. 3486-1**

It is perfect law that governs the direction in which man's choices take him as a free-willed entity.

**For an individual entity with all the attributes of body, soul, and spirit, is subject to the laws thereof; and until individuals are in their thought, purpose, and intent the law—that is constructive—they are subject to same. 1538-1**

**For the law of the Lord is perfect and whatsoever an entity, an individual sows, that must he reap. That as law cannot be changed. As to whether one meets it in the letter of the law or in mercy, in grace, becomes the choice of the entity . . . 5001-1**

The law cannot be changed. That which changes is man's relationship to the law. It is man's choice to live in karma or to live in grace.

. . . **that individuals of their own volition choose the exaltation of self, or the aggrandizement of self's own ego is apparent. This makes for . . . karmic conditions . . . 262-77**

Yet the right effort, the right application of free will makes for conditions of grace.

**[The entity] . . . meets those things which have been called karmic, yet remembering that under the law of grace this may not be other than an urge, and**

that making the will of self one with the Way may prevent, may overcome, may take the choice that makes for life, love, joy, happiness rather than the law that makes, causes the meeting of everything the hard way . . . 1771-2

Each individual constantly meets self. There are no coincidences, no accidents that arise in the meeting of people and individuals . . . 2074-1

Good lives on. The other becomes dross eventually in the experience of each soul . . . 2079-1

For what ye sowed, ye also will reap . . . *It is the law!* The law will not pass away, save as each soul fills, fulfills, same in meting to others that it lacked in other activities . . . 2160-1

. . . these are *experiences* to be met in the entity's application towards conditions as are builded; for as is seen, each and every entity builds that which it, itself, must meet again whether in spoken word, or in act, or deed—for in that builded must the body *meet* its own self. 2750-1

Ye are what ye are because of what ye have been. So is everyone else! 2823-1

And may it finally be remembered:

. . . it is a universal and divine law that like begets like . . . 1472-13

It is a beautiful concept to consider that we as individuals make our own destiny through use of free will. It gives us a responsibility for ourselves and our actions that no other philosophy can attain to. An awesome responsibility indeed! Yet when accepted as a way of living, as a way of application through experiences of life, there comes understanding and awareness of a truly purposed relationship between us and God. With the acceptance of free will in relation to perfect Law the universe becomes a place of co-creation with God.

For man was created a little bit higher than all the

**rest of the whole universe, and is capable of harnessing, directing and enforcing the laws of the universe . . . 5-2**

The ideas of free will and law can be expanded *ad infinitum.* The readings are filled with these concepts.

But perhaps the most comforting concept which the Cayce source presents on this subject is contained in the idea that man is not left alone to discover this free-will relationship to spiritual, mental, and physical laws.

"God has not willed that any soul should perish." The readings state specifically that this is the most important phrase in the Bible. Why is this idea so important? How does it relate to free will?

Man needs a pattern toward which to apply his free will, just as a seamstress needs a pattern to sew a dress. The soul pattern to each man is Jesus Christ.

**For the experience of every soul in the material plane is not mere chance, but the fulfilling of that as was set in motion from the entrance of Spirit into matter, that man may know his true relationship to the Creative Forces.**

**And that exemplified in the life and experience of the Master is the only manner in which such may be known; for only in the manner in which an individual applies self in his relationships to his fellow man is there materially manifested one's concept or one's glorifying of the Maker. 1786-1**

Jesus fulfilled "that set in motion from the entrance of Spirit into matter" on every level of existence—to the perfect glory of God. He fulfilled all laws. He discovered and became the pattern for the true relationship that each man must eventually bear to all laws on all levels.

**He alone is each soul pattern.**

**He *alone* is each soul pattern!**

**He is thy karma *(karma)* if ye put thy trust wholly in Him! See? 2067-2**

We can only begin to realize the significance of this through much effort and study and ultimately only through personal application. We each draw our own conclusions.

*(Q) Please explain, "He, with the cross, represents something in the experience of every entity in their activities through the earth."*

**(A) As we have given, and as was given by Him, in the beginning He was the Son—*made* the Son—those of the Sons that went astray, and through the varying activities overcame the world through the *experiences, bearing* the cross in each and every experience, reaching the *final* cross with *all* power, *all* knowledge, in having overcome the world—and of Himself accepted the Cross . . . 262-36**

Through His many incarnations, Jesus was prepared as the pattern for how we each can fulfill our relationship to the law of like for like—and thereby transform our karma and separation from God into perfect grace and active union with God. Love works love, just as selfishness begets separation from God. Jesus acted consistently in full knowledge of this law by manifesting the perfect Spirit of Christ, the perfect love of the Father God within.

**. . . Hence doing away with that often termed karma, that must be met by all. The immutable law of cause and effect is, as evidenced in the world today, in the material, the mental, and the spiritual world, but He—in overcoming the world, the law— became the law. The law, then, becomes as the school master, or the school of training—and we who have *named* the Name, then are no longer under the law as the law, but under mercy as in Him . . . 262-36**

Jesus is the master. Because He has entered the flesh and acted in the fullness of His relationship to God's laws, we all have access to the Christ Spirit within as joint heirs in sonship to God.

**So, in overcoming all, He set that as the throne, or**

**the mercy seat, that is within the temple, as the pattern, as the mount. 262-36**

Jesus ascended to this mount, to this high place within through activities in a flesh body. The pattern was set "within the temple," not in some intangible ether-world body. The instrument for attaining that pattern is free will. It is our instrument of expression in the material plane; it is that by which we build karma or grace. It is our choice. It is fortunate that we have a pattern by which to govern that choice.

**Karmic influences must ever be met, but He has prepared a way that He takes them upon Himself, and as ye trust in Him, He shows thee the way to meet hindrances or conditions that would disturb thee in any phase of thy experience . . . For karmic forces are:**

**What is meted must be met. If they are met in Him that is the Maker, the Creator of all that is in manifestation as He has promised, then not in *blind* faith is it met—but by the deeds and the thoughts, and the acts of the body, that through Him the conditions may be met day by day . . . Thus has He brought every soul that would trust in Him . . . For, since the foundations of the world He has paved the ways, here and there entering into the experience of man's existence that He may know every temptation that might beset man in all his ways. 442-3**

Jesus, as is the destiny of each man, used free will through many incarnations to express the God Force within, until in perfection He escaped the cyclic pattern of rebirth, beyond all karmic patterns of separation, and became reunited again with the Creative Forces, co-creator with God, one with all force.

**. . . in that as the Christ He came into the earth, fulfilling then that which makes Him that channel that we making ourselves a channel through Him**

may—with the boldness of the Son—approach the throne of mercy and grace and pardon, and know that all that has been done is washed away in that He suffered, that *we* have meted to our brother, in the change that is wrought in our lives, through the manner we act toward him . . . 442-3

What "we have meted to our brother" comes upon us as the daily problems of our individual lives. The Christ Power is available to all in the Christ Pattern, Jesus. He is that opportunity to overcome which lies behind every limiting situation, every troubled condition of our lives. He is our karma.

As to how to meet each problem.

Take it to Jesus. He *is* the answer . . . He is Life, Light, and Immortality. He is Truth, and is thy elder brother . . .

Will ye open and let Him in? For in Him is strength, not in the law, not in the man, not in the multitude of men, nor of conditions or circumstance. For He ruleth, He maketh them every one . . . 1326-1

Grace is assured in Jesus, our elder brother, who has experienced all before us. He has overcome all things through free will. He has chosen wisely. It remains for each man to choose that same pattern in his daily life. It is God's gift to man, the birthright of free will, that enables him to do so. For it is eternally true that God has not willed that any soul should perish, but with every temptation, with every experience possible to man, God has provided the way, the pattern of right action.

That pattern is Jesus Christ.

# Practical Steps to
# Dream Interpretation
♦
## by Marian Little

SCIENTIFIC RESEARCH HAS shown that everyone dreams every night. All dreams have meaning, and the meaning is helpful to the dreamer, according to Edgar Cayce:

**Those [dreams] that make such an impression on the conscious forces as to become a portion of the mental activities . . . should be interpreted. 294-40**

**As we see, all visions and dreams are given for the benefit of the individual, would they but interpret them correctly . . . 294-15**

The purpose here is to give the beginner a practical step-by-step guide to dream interpretation.

## Materials Needed

A spiral notebook has been found practical because it lies flat and makes working in the notebook easier; however, any style of notebook will be fine.

Dreams speak to us in the language of the unconscious symbolism. Every dreamer employs his own individual symbolic language, which often utilizes universal symbolism as well. When we want to study our dreams seriously, it is helpful to compile our own personal dream symbol dictionary. Some use a small loose-leaf notebook with alphabetical index; others prefer a card file. The latter is a little more bulky to carry, but it is easier to index.

And a pencil. Some like a pencil flashlight for writing at night.

## How to Remember Dreams

We need to be prepared with notebook and pencil beside the bed so dreams may be recorded immediately upon awakening. There is detriment in dream recall beginning two minutes after awakening. By eight minutes after awakening the average person has forgotten his dreams. The use of autosuggestion prior to sleep facilitates recall; if we have difficulty remembering dreams it is helpful to say, "I will remember my dreams when I awake in the morning." It is also helpful to write key symbols in the notebook immediately upon awakening so that dream pictures do not slip out of consciousness unrecorded. Household duties, getting to class, going to work may interfere with recording the whole dream right away. If interpretation is postponed, reviewing key symbols usually aids dream recall.

## How to Record Dreams

It is efficient to date the pages the night before and plan to write dreams on one side of a page, leaving the facing page free for work on dream analysis. It is best not to mix the two because the dream will always stand as it has been given us, but interpretations may change.

The dream should be recorded as fully as possible, including such details as people, setting, actions, emotions, colors, numbers, and impressions. What seems to be an unimportant detail could be an important clue to the dream's meaning. Honesty is essential when recording dreams.

**Be honest with thyself, as ye would ask even the ruler of thine earth—the sun—to harken to the voice of that which created it and to give its light *irrespective* of how ye act! 5757-1**

Dream happenings often do not conform to the space-time world.

**The dreams are that, that the entity may gain the more perfect understanding and knowledge of those forces that go to make up the real existence . . . 140-6**

**. . . man seeks [consciousness] for his *own* diversion. In the sleep [the mind of the soul] seeks the *real* diversion, or the *real* activity of self. 5754-3**

The following step is of utmost importance: at the top of the page, briefly record important events of the day before, the main strands of thought, activities, efforts. Dreams are usually a comment on what we have been doing, thinking, praying, and meditating about.

**Sleep—that period when the soul takes stock of that it *has* acted upon during one rest period to another, making or drawing—as it were—the comparisons that make for Life itself in its *essence*, as for harmony, peace, joy, love, long-suffering, patience, brotherly love, kindness—these are the fruits of the Spirit. Hate, harsh words, unkind thoughts, oppressions and the like, these are the fruits of the evil forces, or Satan, and the soul either abhors that it**

**has passed, or enters into the joy of its Lord. 5754-2**

## How to Interpret Dreams

Important symbols should be underlined and then listed separately and interpreted. Each symbol may have several meanings. One of them will best fit the context of the dream. When we cannot think of anything related to the symbol, we can ask ourselves how we would describe this symbol to another person and record that description as a possible meaning. Sometimes simple dictionary definitions provide an answer.

Books and symbol dictionaries may also provide a take-off point to interpretation, if we keep in mind that the meaning of a symbol may be different for us than its denotation.

When we find meanings that fit the dream context, it helps to record that meaning in our own dream dictionary or file. We are then on our way to learning the language of symbolism.

Another approach to unlocking dream meaning is to ask the purpose of the dream as a whole. "What is the dream trying to tell me?" This may be fairly obvious even though we don't understand every symbol in the dream. But let's not forget to take a second look, because dreams are sometimes not as obvious in meaning as we first think they are.

When we find the meaning of one dream of a night, that meaning may be the clue to the other dreams of the same night, which often relate to different aspects of the same subject, as do successive acts in a play.

In order to find the meanings of the symbols, we must think back to the activities, thoughts, and emotions of the previous day. The dream is usually related in some way to yesterday's events unless, as is occasionally the case, the dream is precognitive or an ESP type.

Almost always each person, animal, house, automobile,

and other symbol in the dream represents an aspect of ourselves and our own situation. The main character in the dream is always the dreamer. If we dream of Uncle Joe who talks too much, the dream may be saying that we, like Uncle Joe, talk too much. When we dream of a ferocious lion who is tearing into people, the dream may be saying that we have been destructively tearing into others. When we dream we are in a beautifully furnished, large house, we know the place we live in consciousness, our home, is furnished with beautiful thoughts and expanded awareness. When we dream an automobile is in danger of an accident, we might look to see what is happening that could injure our own physical body, our motor power.

Remembering what we did or thought about the day before, plus knowing that each symbol is an aspect of self, helps unlock the meaning of the dream. This is rather like the process of spotting a forest fire. Two towers are needed, and the direction from each tower is coordinated to spot the exact location.

Dreams are invented by each of us as messages from self to self. Each person is his own best interpreter.

. . . wake to the realization that "the Spirit beareth witness with my spirit" and the answer comes from within and must ever come from within. Not in the thunder, not in the whirlwind, not in the storm, nor any of the mighty ravings . . . of nature, whether of the material forces or of the mental ravings that may shadow or be overshadowed, but ever the still small voice that answers to self . . . 900-66

This reading implies that we should dare to think as highly of self as our dreams say we should. However, there are many times when we need to be courageous enough to admit that there is room for improvement, God knows all already, and our friends may have been too kind to tell us.

. . . it is the individual's job, each individual's condition, each individual's position, each individual's

**relation, each individual's manifestation, each individual's receiving the message from the higher forces themselves, and for each individual to understand if they will study, to show themselves approved. 3744-5**

An element of practicality is necessary in interpretation. When we dream of eating fish, it may mean exactly what it says. Eat fish. If we dream of an automobile accident, it may not be about health. The dream may be suggesting greater care in driving.

A word of caution: Edgar Cayce said that dreams could be helpful if interpreted correctly. If a dream seems to be telling us to do something which we know is not constructive, we have probably misinterpreted the dream.

**Do not consider so much what others should do for or to *you*, but what will you do for and towards others. And realize that all of these must be constructive in their nature. 1889-1**

## Some Examples

1. A middle-aged mother dreamed her *daughter* was driving a car in the driveway of their home, headed toward the street. It was a *compact car.* The daughter *spun the wheels forward.* The *car wouldn't move* because it was in a *patch of ice and snow.* There were *sparks and noise of wheels spinning.* The daughter then spun the wheels to *go backward.* The car *lurched backward* and sped toward a *row of trees.* The mother observing from *upstairs* in the house thought the daughter was going to *hit the trees,* but the daughter *put the brakes on* just in time.

Daughter—the main character of the dream, therefore representing an aspect of the mother. The daughter is honest, impetuous, and fifteen years old.

Compact car—a car often represents the body; the mother had been on a successful diet.

Spun wheels forward—the mother wanted to make progress quickly.

Car wouldn't move—mother unable to get anywhere.

Patch of ice and snow—a cold and frozen area in consciousness which keeps the mother from making progress.

Sparks and noise of wheels spinning—the mother has a temper, she "spins her wheels."

Go backward; lurched backward—when progress was not made, the mother went backward, became negative in attitude.

Row of trees; hit the trees—this person likes trees; they represent growth to her, growth over a long period of time.

Upstairs—the mother's view of the scene from a higher level of consciousness.

Put the brakes on—the brakes of a car may represent willpower; this woman used willpower to stop her negative way of thinking.

Analysis: The day before, the mother had asked her doctor for information about her health. He responded coldly and was not helpful. The woman, unable to get anywhere with her questions, became angry and negative. Then she realized that this would hurt only herself, and she used willpower to stop negative thinking.

2. A *young woman* dreamed she was being *led up broad stairs* by an *older woman* to the *apartment* of a very creative person. The stair hall was lined with *white marble* containing streaks of *gold*. The *stair rail* was of *burnished brass*. The older woman was going *up on her knees, sideways*. She said, *"This is the only way you can do it."* The young woman said, "That is too hard for me," and was planning simply to walk up the stairs.

Young woman—the main character, the dreamer.

Led up broad stairs—the dreamer is being led to a higher level of consciousness.

Older woman—an older, more mature part of the dreamer.

Apartment—an apartment is shared with other people

(consideration for others); an apartment is part of a larger building (development of one aspect of the dreamer's whole life).

White marble; gold—surrounding self with purity and spirituality.

Stair rail—that which is grasped to maintain balance.

Burnished brass—brass denotes understanding (meaning obtained from symbol dictionary); burnishing and polishing is applying a lot of work, application.

Up on her knees—humility.

Sideways—approaching creativeness indirectly, through development of other constructive character traits.

"This is the only way you can do it"—a direct quote from an "authority figure," part of the dreamer herself, an important person to listen to.

Analysis: The young woman wanted to develop an artistic talent. She could do it only in one way—by maintaining balance in her personality, in humility, much application, by surrounding herself with purity and God's spirit, and by consideration of those who lived with her. It would be difficult.

## How to Obtain Guidance from Dreams

Dreams guide and help us after we set goals and ideals for our lives. Obviously, these we must choose carefully.

**. . . there must be the choice of ideals, spiritually, mentally, materially. These should not be merely as tenets that you will think about or that you would copy from a prayer book or even from the Book itself, the Bible. But rather as the result of the entity "thinking same through" but referring to at least ten promises of the Lord and Master. Find these, yes. 5322-1**

Our choices may or may not coincide with those set for us by parents, mate, or friends.

The *individual is accountable in self* as to what its ideas, purposes or ideals are, and is *not* to be dominated or persuaded, or forced, through any condition, to give even a purpose, or word, toward other than its *individual* ideal and purpose concerning same—for, as has been given, God created man in his own image, and gave, "I have set before thee—this day—good and evil. Choose *thou* whom thou will serve, whether the ideals as are set in His way and Spirit, or the desires of the flesh." 257-20

Be sure you are right, then go ahead . . . Study to show thyself approved unto God. That is why the injunction, know thy ideals. Know the Author of thy hopes, and thy purposes. 3226-1

Choices usually require serious self-examination. What do we really want our goals to be? What do we want our place in the world to be? When we make wrong choices, our dreams will surely tell us. When we wander through life without goals, our dreams wander right along with us with only an occasional prod. "If we are choosing the highest, the best, we will not be satisfied with anything less. It is well for us to remember that the highest goal is not reached at a single bound, but step by step—here a little, there a little." *(A Search for God, Book 1)* It is well for us to move toward our ideals with one-step-at-a-time goals, making each step practical and reachable. Growth of the highest quality takes a long, long time. An oak tree grows slowly and steadily in beauty and strength to fullness and fruition.

Prayer aids in obtaining guidance.

Seek and ye shall find. Know in whom thou hast believed, and believe—in faith—He is able to commit that *thou* hast committed unto Him against *any* condition in thine experience. *Thy* will, O Lord, be done, not mine! *Ask*—leave the result with Him. His promises are sure. "Heaven and earth may pass away,

but my promises shall *not* pass away." 262-17
Meditation practiced regularly will clear the channels
to receive guidance.

The more that there is held that the mental and
physical body is surrounded by, is protected by, that
consciousness of the Master that gave, "I will not
leave thee comfortless," and the greater the physical can be submerged, the greater will be the activity of the spiritual forces in and through such bodies.
281-5
We should apply in our daily lives the advice available.

Dreams come to this body [Edgar Cayce], as to other
individuals, so that . . . the body-consciousness—applying same—may gain the better understanding of
conditions as they arise. And these—applied in the
way and manner designated through the various experiences or visions of conditions as presented—will
prove beneficial, and should be followed closely. 294-
105
As ye apply, as ye make use of that in hand, more
is given thee. For, day unto day is sufficient, if use is
made thereof . . . 1206-13
The application of our interpretation of the dream is its
true interpretation.

Take not of that which is new until weighed well
with that which has been lived and is true, see? While
these forces give the truth, the life, the light, this
[information] also may be used only as the developments of same, with the individual, are carried to
that point, see?

The understanding that is finally shown gives then
reliance that must be put in the work as its own self
. . . rather than depending upon the interpretation of
same by the mental, physical mind, see?

That is, the best interpretation of God is God, the
best interpretation of truth is truth, by the light of

**that accomplished in same, see? 294-39**

It is helpful to go back over dreams occasionally after we are separated in time and emotion from them. Sometimes we are able to see more clearly in retrospect. Meanings become apparent we had not seen; symbols gain depth. It helps to record symbol definitions as we go along day by day in our individual dream dictionary.

Another aid to dream interpretation is a close friend or a small group, such as a Search for God Study Group. Sometimes others know us better than we do ourselves. We may think we do not have the unused talent or characteristic a dream says we have. Sometimes our friends know we do. A friend or a group helps not by forcing interpretations on the dreamer, but by simply asking if he thinks a symbol or dream could mean this or that. It is the dreamer's dream, and in the final analysis, he has the last word.

**. . . the understanding for the individual entity, viewed from its own standpoint, with its knowledge, is obtained and made ready by itself, to be manifested through itself, towards its own development . . . 3744-5**

## Sharing with Others

It is essential, when we have found a portion of the "living water," to share it with others who also seek the "living way."

**Give of self, of body, of mind, to the developing of self and others . . . let the will become subjugated to the will of the Father, that such knowledge as gained through dream, manifestation, vision, may be given to a dying world, and give that people who would approach the living way, the living water, and may they be again established in the holy way that leads to everlasting; giving the inmost feelings, the inmost**

life, a feeling such as makes the countenance, the physical exhibition of body, of mind, such as all who behold may know *this one* has approached the throne and brought away the shining light, ever the light by night and the cloud by day; presenting self in that manner that all manifestations will become in the way that will lend strength, shrouding doubt, fear, disappointments, distrust, in the depths such a way that only the true, the holy light, will shine unto the end, guiding many to the way that leads to life ever-lasting. 900-13

# Creativity in Everyday Living:
## An Approach from *A Search for God*

### by Martin Apelman

THERE HAS BEEN considerable study and investigation of the subject of creativity—some of it scientific, some philosophical, the majority of it psychological. Most of the research has been behavioral in its approach; that is, it has gone after the effects of creativity, but very little of it has come up with the causes and conditions for developing creativity. Almost none of it has approached creativity as an everyday experience.

There is one analysis, however, which treats creativity in almost all of its aspects and manifestations, including its everyday application. That analysis is the book by Dr. Harmon Bro, entitled *Edgar Cayce on Religion and Psychic Experience*. I have drawn freely from that book for this article.

According to many of Edgar Cayce's readings, creativity in man is a gift from the Creative Forces, or God. Man once found creative ability more readily available to him than he does now. He was not an early anthropoid at that time; he was at that point in Creation, a soul with the freedom to roam the universe and create playfully with the rest of the cosmos. Intense thought, through soul energies, objectified realms of beauty and form.

Then, millions of souls explored the limits of their energies too far, produced grotesqueries, and trapped themselves in the matter which they had objectified. By so doing, they rejected their abilities to be co-creators with God.

To help these self-snared souls rediscover their originally endowed creative energies (and prevent further barbarisms against themselves and the physical world which they had objectified) they were given their own evolutionary process. They were programmed to reincarnate in a succession of varying human forms, interspersing lifetimes in other planes of consciousness in order to build qualities that would help reinstate them to their original nature.

The human-form experiences are opportunities to practice what is learned in those other planes of consciousness. In human form, psychic and creative energies are harder for some of us to tap into, but they are still there in all of us, and they are part of the same Creative Force that endowed them in the beginning.

But how do we tap into those inner creative energies in everyday life, and how can they manifest themselves?

There are energy fields that are part of and surround each human form, as well as everything else. These fields have complex patterns of vibrations that are generated by the One Force. When the energy fields of the human psyche or soul are set into phase with another field "out there somewhere," the result is a psychic perception.

When that energy field is charged between the two poles of attunement and service, the result is creative energy.

Creativity, in its broadest sense, is the soul's entering into events (through attunement) in such ways that the consequences are other events, each working to fulfill the promise of shared human existence (service). Creativity, thus, can be as little as not forgetting to water a garden or brewing a pot of coffee for an unexpected visitor, or as big as writing the Declaration of Independence or painting the *Mona Lisa.*

Real creativity can exist in every dimension of life, providing the two poles of attunement and service are present and emitting their energy fields.

The problem of all creativity is the ability to stimulate and to tolerate the flow of relevant material from the unconscious to the conscious, delaying a selection from that material until the most likely options are identified, and then following them through to completion. For this process, a certain playfulness, humor, and tentativeness is needed, with an ability to endure the strain of no ready solution and a drive to finish up and follow through.

To be creative, whether it be on the colossal scale of Beethoven's Ninth Symphony or on the microscale of hammering the right nail in the right place, often involves a suspension of judgment in the trust that a solution will present itself. It involves a commitment to take action on a tentative solution in the trust that such an action will be worthwhile. It involves an ability to overhaul one's functioning after repeated failures, in the trust that eventually one can arrive at a better pattern of problem-solving.

The issue comes up time and again—what can man trust when habit, experience, counsel, or expedience all fail to offer solutions?

The answer to that should lead to an attempt to outline the essential conditions for effective creativity in an everyday, practical living experience.

From the Cayce source, it is learned that these conditions are what men have sought to understand and practice through what they call religion. The function of those organized rituals, sacraments, codes, commandments was to focus and train man's energies into alignment with the Creative Forces we call God, so as to produce a flow of new and abundant creations, through attunement and service.

This quest for creativity, and the effective conditions for it, however, must be made over and over again—by each generation, by each individual soul. Man has free will in his creativity, and often chooses self-seeking and self-serving rather than an expression of his real relation to the ultimate Source of good.

A group of Edgar Cayce's friends asked for lessons in spiritual development through his readings. They started out being interested in developing some measure of psychic ability, which Cayce had demonstrated in helping them. What they received were lessons in establishing the major conditions of creativity in daily living. There were twenty-four such lessons, later published in two books called *A Search for God.*

The first lesson is the question of belonging, called "Cooperation." It is concerned with the relationships one seeks from raising a child to running a business. This is not using people, as Erich Fromm called "symbiosis," where two needy people use each other but never really relate as human beings. In modern psychiatry, the emphasis on group therapy stresses belonging as the basis for creative relationships.

Cooperation doesn't mean merely joining a group or a church without relating to others in service, an action which produces its own energy. Perhaps this is what was meant by "where two or three are gathered together in my name, there am I in the midst of them." (Matt. 18:20) Cooperation, in the Cayce sense, is the embodiment of those two energy poles mentioned before: service and attunement.

Cayce said many times in his readings, "Don't just be good, be good *for something.*" This was his source's basis for creativity in every dimension of life. Service without attunement is do-goodism, which is using others for your own advantage.

The Cayce readings suggest that cooperation is the fully creative mode of belonging, and the starting point for the development of all talents or gifts.

The second lesson in cultivating conditions for creativity is self-analysis. The second chapter of *A Search for God* is "Know Thyself," which is what the ancient Delphic Oracle offered repeatedly. No school of psychology or psychiatry disagrees with this precept. Many studies of creative individuals have consistently shown that the more creative a person is, the more *typically* he has access to his inward life. This includes his motives, his emotions, fantasies, drives, energies—a fairly accurate appraisal of his own strengths and weaknesses. Self-knowledge and self-acceptance are what David Reisman says is the difference between the "autonomous," well-adjusted man and ill-adjusted or over-adjusted man.

Good adjustment permits a flow of hunches, intuitions, and impressions *that one can trust.* Maladjustment tends to turn off the promptings of the psyche or soul, or turn on a flow of material from the less desirable realms of consciousness. Incidentally, the definition of *intuition* is learning from within.

Beethoven learned to use intuition as part of his development. J.W.N. Sullivan in his book, *Beethoven, His Spiritual Development*, states: "Beethoven's music is an example of the path of spiritual development with greater and greater reliance on leadings from within—not consciously in its self-regard but aware of those leadings and following them unrelentingly." He also writes that

Beethoven's passionate conviction about the nature of his intuitions was best expressed in the mystical sentences he copied from Eastern literature. A phrase which he had framed and kept on his desk was, "I am that which is. I am all that was, that is, and that shall be."

The Cayce readings relate the first two conditions of creativity—cooperation and self-knowledge. Cooperation stresses the bending of the individual will to serve God in the other person through an awareness of one's real self, as well as the overcoming of the self-ignorance that may impede that cooperation. Without both knowledge and self-knowledge, efforts to cooperate may become either a maudlin sentimentalizing or totalitarianism, both in the name of a misconceived deity.

The self-analysis referred to involves an investigation of the inescapable relationship of the body, the mind, and the soul. The self-knowing of body, mind, and soul is not gauged by what a man has, but rather by what he gives.

The third area considered essential for creativity is the general area of conscience. In *A Search for God*, this chapter is entitled "What Is My Ideal?" Conscience has been the subject of a great deal of attention in classical and neo-classical psychology and psychiatry. The Rohrschach ink blot tests and the projective card and drawing techniques show how individuals perceive situations according to their subconscious patterns. What we perceive in others lies somewhere on the axis of our own conscience structure. A large part of psychotherapy is a re-evaluation of the conscience control system, trying to bring it in line with the limits imposed by a given culture.

There are many terms used for conscience: the Freudian "superego" concept, the "guiding fictions" of Adler, the "dominant archetypes" of Jung, or the Erich Fromm "fatherly-motherly" conscience. Regardless of what it is called, conscience development and operation hold a critical place in therapy and education theory.

The Cayce source, in approaching ideals or conscience as a condition for creativity, addressed the question of relating God's controls to man's. This is an old question, but it is also as modern as one's stand regarding war, contraception, capital punishment, or permissive child rearing.

In this, the readings make a clear distinction between "ideas" and "ideals." An idea is a unit of mental activity, stimulated by the needs of the body or by the soul. It is created by the imagination and the heart of man and it may or may not be in line with his ideal. The ideal, on the other hand, is a pattern-giving structure which is in the character of the soul-energies available to man. One can welcome these energies and use them positively, negatively, or ignore them. Free will comes into play here in a significant way.

The ideals we hold and live by are capable of unleashing enormous creative energies, for positive creation if handled properly or for negative creation if misapplied. This suggests a way of living, not by a book of rules or taboos or formulas, but by identifying with the Christ as a personal challenge rather than as a hero.

The fourth condition for creativity is initiative, covered in the chapter entitled "Faith" in *A Search for God.* No creativity ever took place without a commitment to some kind of action (be it mental or physical). That commitment is an initiative which is based on a trust that a solution will present itself. That trust is what the Cayce source called "faith."

The readings indicate that Creative Energies (God) cannot help a man until he is in action. The point seems to be, "Don't just sit there, do *something.*"

Faith, through initiative, is described as a flow of promptings with definite content, coming into the conscious mind from the subconscious. When we learn to recognize that flow and respond to it in an action that radiates the energy set up between service and attunement, we have the beginnings of some pretty powerful creativity.

The readings also affirm that faith is not an all-or-nothing affair. It comes gradually as we learn how to get rid of the blocks to that flow, which are mostly centered about the self or ego. Perhaps that's what is meant by, "Lord, I believe; help thou mine unbelief." (Mark 9:24)

On the question of faith, a few distinctions have to be learned by each of us according to his own patterns: the difference between faith and unconscious compulsions, and the difference between faith and imagination. The Cayce material offers us direction in developing criteria for distinguishing between the promptings of faith and other promptings.

The fifth essential for cultivating creativity is integrity, the two components of which are the subject of the fifth lesson in *A Search for God*, "Virtue and Understanding." Integrity, as a condition for creativity, becomes a behavioral concept; virtue is behavior that is consistent with the highest motives, which allows a flow of insights that makes for understanding, leading in turn to more effective behavior. It becomes a beautiful cycle of energy feedback.

There is no doubt that personal integrity affects the creative activity of an individual. The absence of a personal integrity can lead to a will to fail or it can produce self-righteousness.

Psychological investigations have shown that creativity in problem solving and in the arts has not always shown a high correlation with the *public* norms of virtue. When *inner* convictions, however, are measured against creative productivity, a different picture appears.

Part of the job of developing integrity is to make sure that personality is in line with individuality. Personality, according to the Cayce source, is a man's public self—all the trappings with which he surrounds himself in order to reinforce the image he asks the world to accept of him. Individuality, however, is the sum total of what has been done in accord with our ideals.

It is the individuality that all of us seek to know, so that we can eventually drop away those aspects of personality that are not consistent with the individuality. The cultivation of integrity is a continuous thing, and the best way to start is simply to try.

The sixth condition for creativity is the radical acceptance of others, discussed in the "Fellowship" chapter in *A Search for God.* This condition requires that man approach all others with an acceptance that goes beyond an uncritical identification or an unqualified rejection. Martin Buber has written eloquently of acceptance as the "I-Thou" relation. He prefers to use Thou rather than It; otherwise, the other person would become an abstraction that we use for our convenience. In Buber's terms, we realize our fullest selves when we are fully accepting in our relations with others, no matter how fleeting that relationship.

By contrast, when we only partially relate to others, or don't relate at all, we are only partly ourselves and reduce our creativity accordingly.

Studies of the psychology of creativity have accepted the factor of attitudes toward others, even though the others may not be involved in the actual creative act. Self-justification is one of those attitudes that is a block to creativity. It is a burden that we place on ourselves that robs us of the flow of insights.

The Cayce source also claimed that no man should be approached as "self-made." All men (and the readings are clear about all men) are of a seed planted at the same time by the One Creative Force. Their very existence should command respect, even if they have to be avoided at times. What this lesson is saying to us is, "Yes, we are our brother's keeper and the very next man we meet that needs help is our brother." Compare that to the statement of some pseudo-philosophers who claim they love mankind but can't stand people.

To be one's brother's keeper means more than cheering him on from a safe distance. The readings imply that the nearest house of God to where we stand is the next human flesh. This suggests that even when thinking of our enemies, we can't settle for just thinking positive thoughts, but must come to a real yearning for others to fulfill the promise of their being. This is not sympathy, nor is it overlooking shortcomings, but rather is a *total* response of love for which we can call on the Christ, that He may show us how to pray.

This is part of the cooperation stage of creativity. In the view of the Cayce source, this does not come from will alone but from calling on our *Elder* Brother, as the one brother who has reached the pinnacle.

How does one begin this radical acceptance that is true fellowship? Self-evaluation is one essential, not to be confused with self-condemnation, which is as dangerous as condemning someone else. Self-condemnation may be a subtle defense against the responsibility for one's life and an ill-advised attempt to placate God with a sacrifice that is not approved by Him.

One of the problems of creativity mentioned earlier was the ability to handle the *stress* of the creative process. This is the subject of the next lesson, "Patience." Studies of the creative process by psychologists have identified endurance of unresolved tension as a hallmark of the creative problem-solver. The creative person is notably one who can "sweat out" productive solutions. He may go to the movies, go to sleep, pray. He may try possible solutions from time to time, not being afraid of making mistakes, but he won't settle for just any solution simply to get it over with. He'll make his move into a right solution when he feels the problem has moved into the solution stage.

This kind of tenacity is based on patience, which is the basis of the ability to withstand stress. It comes into play in composing music, making wood joints in carpentry, solving mathematical equations, trying a new recipe, or for a bachelor learning to sew on a button that stays put. Most people handle stress through a combination of skills and defenses in what is called "ego strength" or the capacity to endure insecurity. When unconscious mechanisms like rationalizations or repressions dominate, the helpful flow of the unconscious seems to be distorted. The psyche is a self-regulating system, and therefore it seems likely that frantic, emotional efforts to solve problems are as self-defeating as the tendency to avoid any problems at all. It seems that the best posture is to stand ready to tackle almost anything that comes along.

The picture of patience, as it appears in the Cayce readings, is, therefore, not one of passivity, but one of active alignment with a timing that is a gift from God to the soul of man. Patience then becomes another dimension for growth. We should like to leap into a position of being "saved" by a single act or decision, but things just don't work that way. Babies don't leap into manhood. It is a process of step by step, "line upon line, precept upon precept." The outlook of the Cayce source is that creation is for keeps; it need not nor can it be rushed or anxious.

Patience is not synonymous with detachment, either. It is an apt response, in God's own timing. To cultivate patience requires that we live a life in proper balance, marked by some whistling, teasing, playing, joking, and seeing the ridiculous in things. In the perspective of the readings, the more one focuses on being alive, in every positive direction, right now, the closer one comes to the real meaning of patience.

The eighth condition in the development of creativity is productivity, dealt with in "The Open Door." Productivity here is not a quantity concept. It refers, rather, to one's ability to maintain a consistent effort to be of practical, useful service to others, and to enlist the help of the Christ Spirit in this effort, keeping the "door" open so that Spirit can enter. We are again at the service-attunement foundation of creativity.

Erich Fromm has described productivity as one of the two ways in which a mature individual can make a meaningful closure with life and with other people—the other way is loving. He also believes that cooperation in productivity offers a better framework for developing all kinds of positive creativity than does competition.

The Cayce information emphasizes God's incredible helpfulness in man's productivity along creative lines. This does not refer to miracles. The Creative Forces are always at work in their productivity, seeking man's full becoming as co-creator. The regularity, the dependability of the Energy, is an assurance that is not a passing marvel.

The "open door" is the readiness of the human body to respond to divine promptings, if the purpose of that help is service and not selfishness.

Self-training in productivity begins with the expectancy of resolutions to problems—how one might approach a job to be done or a relationship that needs settling. Finding productivity means learning the conditions under which one can become caught up in a task to which he responds in a kind of positive excitement.

Both books of *A Search for God* stress meditation. Researchers into creativity have studied the process of "incubation" in which an individual programs his mind with a problem and then waits for the solution to present itself. Conventional psychology has rarely studied the effects of meditation and prayer in the creative process, because that requires some assumptions about the nature of man, soul, and God which, to the ultra-scientific mind, smacks of a medieval view of the world and some sort of magic.

Despite that view, there are hints from many creative people that meditation and prayer might be highly effective in freeing creativity. Meditation and prayer may act as a confirmation to an individual of his own identity and strength, necessary in facing a difficult problem and enduring the strain of waiting for an answer. The meditative process may also lower one's defenses, which in themselves tend to block the flow of unconscious material into consciousness. The process may also help by turning the individual to his highest values.

The question may be asked of one's self—can meditation and prayer be critical for the development of any form of creativity—such as the marketing of a new product, the handling of a political issue, the writing of a letter long overdue, the sewing of a dress from an untried pattern, the amount of spending money to give to a child? One of the hallmarks of the highest creativity appears to be that the solutions presented take account of the needs of all concerned, not just the creator.

The chapter in Book I entitled "In His Presence" treats meditation and prayer in their broader context of being a condition for creativity. It begins with the insistence that unless the God Force is looked for in play, in study, or in work, it will not be found in worship. The thought is that the same channels of energy are operative in the action of the autonomic nervous system on the endocrine glands as are operative in all of man's creative activity. In fact, meditation itself may be considered as a highly creative act— its own form of conception and birth in consciousness.

Prayer, according to the Cayce source, is "the concerted effort of the physical consciousness to become attuned to the Creator . . . *Meditation is emptying* self of all that hinders the creative forces from rising along the natural channels of the physical man to be disseminated through those centers and sources that create the activities of the physical, the mental, the spiritual man." (281-13) Meditation is an individual process, and we can expect almost anything from it if a real inward action is taking place; from feeling currents along the spine, to a heightening of sexual energies, to tears of joy for feeling the incredible goodness of God to give Himself to man.

One can't seek His Presence in meditation if one doesn't try to feel His creative presence in daily activities—buying groceries, pruning plants, making a speech, running a vacuum cleaner, or supporting a drunk. His Presence is either in all of Creation or in none of it.

The next dimension in creativity is sacrifice, outlined in "The Cross and the Crown." The question arises, what has sacrifice to do with creativity? Well, if there is a tendency in all men to orient the ego to a Super-Self below the surface of his consciousness, then the sacrifice of self-will might affect the flow of all kinds of creativity. This kind of sacrifice calls for acting without self-justification or self-defense. That was exactly the kind of sacrifice made in the life and work of Jesus the Christ. The "cross" was followed by the "crown"—the sacrifice followed by companionship with the Father.

The Cayce readings state that crosses are not punishments, they are opportunities to demonstrate our right relation with matter, with the flesh. Further, each man determines his own crosses; he brings them to himself. These are necessary for growth and not always in agreement with the optimism expressed in some psychic circles which claim that all a man has to do is to master occult powers and he can have anything he wants. In other words, a man has to earn his creativity through growth. That earning is giving up some falsely cherished ideals, which at times seems like a cross to bear and is a genuine sacrifice. That kind of sacrifice is not any greater than the fetus leaving the womb—it's a shock, but it's not destruction; as a matter of fact, it's the beginning of life.

These sacrifices or crosses are not always because of or for oneself. They may be necessary so that we can better learn how to help another.

The next condition for creativity is that of trying to polarize thought and action in the struggle against dualism.

The chapter title, "The Lord Thy God Is One," comes from the heart of the Jewish prayer of faith—*Shema Yisroel, Adonoi Elohenu, Adonoi Echod.*

How can dualism, or a split between matter and spirit, between reason and revelation affect creativity in everyday living? Carl Jung has suggested that most dualisms are rooted in an unhealthy separation of ego from a deeper Self. If he is correct, then a strong dualism in a person would tend to break up the harmony of the conscious and the unconscious. This harmony appears necessary in creativity, so that each can stimulate and nurture the other.

It is necessary for the human mind to be polarized, to be singular, toward the One Creative Force at work for maximum creativity. If we can't learn to find the One God in cooking and serving a meal to anybody who needs it, we're not going to find God in a church or a temple.

To call God "One" requires some rethinking of God in terms of force substances that flow and interact and interrelate in an astounding Unity. Like everything else in creativity, however, the discovery of this Oneness of Creative Energy comes a little at a time. The light of this realization is said to be so intense, that if man were to be exposed to it, it would be blinding. Some creative people have been exposed to more than a little in one flash of ideas, and they have described it as so real and so powerful that they felt they almost had to duck and raised their arms in self-protection.

It's a good idea, however, not to wait around for this kind of flash to hit us. Probably the best way to start polarizing our consciousness is to begin acting it out in any little way we can.

If asked to name the elements of human creativity, many would probably start with love, which is the subject of the twelfth and last chapter of Book I of *A Search for God.* Only by starting with cooperation, self-analysis, and the other conditions for creativity, accompanied by prayer and meditation and a growth in patience and sacrifice, can the subject of love be approached. By that time, no surface attraction nor vague goodwill would pass for love.

The Cayce information described love as a healing force. It is not a social invention nor a convenience of relationships; it is an attribute of soul. Love is a force which acts as directly as one musical tone producing its harmonics. This is why some families or work groups or study groups have such a potential for good, creative relationships.

This same force applies to the Christ's command, "Thou shalt love thy neighbor as thyself." (Matt. 22:39) This means one has to start loving by having a regard for his own soul and his own growth before one can feel the same for a neighbor.

The Cayce readings make it clear: " . . . *fulfill* the law of love. Love *is* law, law *is* love, to those that love *His* appearing." (694-2)

# The God Within

*by Janis Davidson*

. . . AS YE GIVE, **as ye do unto thy fellow man ye are doing unto the God in thyself . . . 887-3**

We must come to the conscious realization that God indeed exists within us and is always there. We do not have to go to holy mountains or holy places, for the kingdom of heaven is truly at hand, the place where we are is holy ground—for God, the Divine nature, dwells within at all times.

But often God is kept as an "imprisoned splendor" and His great energy and blessings are not allowed to pour from within us to our brother. How little we realize that by keeping this power confined we are not only denying this blessing to others but also denying it to ourselves. For as we let flow from within us the attributes of God—the fruits, the effects of the Spirit—we ourselves experience these effects just as much as does the person to whom the blessing is directed because these attributes of God are permeating our very being as we allow them to flow from the God within to the world outside.

For example, when a situation calls forth from us an overwhelming feeling of love and compassion toward someone, we are also an integral part and are consciously experiencing this feeling even more strongly than the person toward whom we have expressed it. Becoming aware of this enables us to experience its truth. Thus, by being a channel of blessing toward others, truly are we also recipients of the blessing. All is One. No wonder it is said that it should be a joy to us to be about our Father's business!

On the other hand, when we choose to keep this splendor imprisoned within us and instead use our wills to express negative and destructive qualities such as hatred, we experience the feeling and the quality and the emotional involvement with hatred as much as, or even more than, the person to whom that emotion is directed. In expressing hatred over and over, it is the person expressing it who must live with this hatred and who might even see this attitude manifested on the physical level as disease. When we express that negative quality, it is a part of us, it permeates our being—and it is done to the God within. It might not be our intention to subject God to negative attitudes, to have Him live in the midst of them, but in actuality this is what occurs.

How do we really want to act toward our God? We answer this in each of our thoughts and each of our actions.

**The ways may be set before thee—the *choices* must be *taken* of thine own consciousness. Be aware of what ye would that the Lord would do with thee, what *thou* would do with the opportunities, the privileges He hath bestowed upon thee as one of His children. 1470-2**

We should remember that we have only by giving, for we can have and experience God's love, gentleness, mercy, serenity as we allow these qualities to flow through us by releasing them from the God center within ourselves.

# Gearing the Body for the Aquarian Age

## by Lawrence M. Steinhart

MOST OF US are aware of the psychic evolution coming about in the Aquarian Age, and many of us are increasingly aware of the spiritual promises which are unfolding in the human race. However, few of us are taking practical steps toward preparing our bodies, the vehicles through which we have earthly expressions, for the changes that are also to come in the physical world. It is within the body, the temple of the living God, that we must meet God face to face.

The sleeping Cayce, as sages before him, advised seeking the way within oneself. "It is *within* that there is the kingdom of heaven!" (877-27) According to the readings, the man Jesus—who became the Christ—was and is a pattern of the way in which man can develop to his ultimate purpose.

Lifetime after lifetime man wonders "what is my ultimate purpose?" Pursuing the answer to this question he evolves, but in that evolvement makes some mistakes. Often the same mistake is made repeatedly. Recurring habit patterns build what might be termed the "karmic chain," a whole series of related mistakes. One's own habits are difficult to recognize; knowing oneself can be a painful experience, but necessary for the evolution to the next level of consciousness. Enslaved by our karmic chains, we seek to break out via the weakest link, which for many of us is the appetite.

## Diet

The readings frequently recommended that one should eat foods grown or produced in the vicinity in which the individual resides. In this way he could acclimatize himself to the vibrations of the area. In today's world of polluted, synthesized, and unnatural foods, Cayce's words are especially valid. Foods which ripen naturally and are eaten where they are grown are always preferable to exotic luxuries shipped from "faraway places with strange-sounding names." For, as the readings stated:

**Shipped vegetables are never very good. 2-14**

**Have *most* of the foods that are grown in the area where the body lives, as much as practical. 337-27**

**Use fruits, nuts, berries of all natures or characters that are grown in the environ of the body . . . 1773-3**

**. . . plenty of both raw and well-cooked vegetables, and those that are grown the more in the environ in which the body finds itself. 2066-2**

This is a good reason to sprout beans and seeds at home, because not only are sprouts high in vitamins and minerals, but also they are the most easily digested form of vegetable protein. Absolutely fresh from the sprouter, their vitality is undiminished. One half cup of sprouted soybeans contains the same amount of vitamin C as six glasses of orange juice.

Most people know that cooking vegetables lessens their vitamin and mineral value. Despite the glamour of the jet-age kitchen (microwave ovens, Teflon-coated pans, and instant frozen gourmet dishes), eating cooked food is still second best. However, if we *must* cook it, we might consider preparing it in cooking parchment (Patapar Paper was referred to in the readings), in its own natural juices. This has the Cayce seal of approval as has the pressure cooker:

*(Q) Consider also the steam pressure for cooking foods quickly. Would it be recommended and does it destroy any of the precious vitamins of the vegetables and fruits?*

**(A) Rather preserves than destroys. 462-14**

**We would include the Jerusalem artichoke in the diet . . . cooked in its own juices—that is, in Patapar Paper, so that all the juice of same may be stirred or mixed with the bulk when this is eaten. 243-36**

**. . . the preferable way to prepare [the vegetable] juices would be through cooking the vegetables after tying them in Patapar Paper; not putting them in water to boil, but cooking either in the Patapar Paper or in a steam steamer, so that only the juices from the vegetables may be obtained—and no water added in the cooking at all . . . A little later the body may begin with stewed chicken, or broiled chicken or broiled fish . . . [Even] the chicken or fish would be better cooked in the Patapar Paper or a steam cooker. 133-4**

People are waking up to the fact that aluminum changes the chemistry of certain foods prepared in it. More and more we are switching to stainless steel, enamel, and porcelain pots. We are using steamers for our vegetables so that the vitamin content doesn't run down the drain. But Cayce's recommendation for the use of a cooking parchment is still the method which delivers a greater amount of nutriments. This is not a complicated affair, and it is also economical as the parchment can be used over and over again.

The readings further suggest that condiments should be used *after* the cooking of foods.

**The cooking of condiments, even salt, *destroys* much of the vitamins of foods. 906-1**

The regular use of gelatin was advised. It was suggested that raw vegetables and salads be prepared in a gelatin mold, making sure that none of the juices escape. Because gelatin is obtained from animal cartilage, vegetarians may prefer to use Agar Agar flakes, which are derived from seaweed. It is not the vitamin content in the gelatin itself which is so important but rather its acting as a catalyst.

*(Q) Please explain the vitamin content of gelatin. There is no reference to vitamin content on the package.*

**(A) It isn't the vitamin content but it is ability to work with the activities of the glands, causing the glands to take from that absorbed or digested the vitamins that would not be active if there is not sufficient gelatin in the body. See, there may be mixed with any chemical that which makes the rest of the system susceptible or able to call from the system that needed. It becomes then, as it were, "sensitive" to conditions. Without it there is not that sensitivity. 849-75**

Red meat is to be eaten rarely (excuse the pun); the meats preferred in the readings are lamb, poultry, and fish. They explain that, unless one is extremely active and able to "work off" the energy created by the red meat, the excess would act as a dross in the system.

In the diet keep away from red meats, ham, or rare steak or roasts. Rather use fish, fowl and lamb. 3596-1

And in the manner of diet, keep away from too much grease or too much of any foods cooked in quantities of grease—whether it be the fat of hog, sheep, beef or fowl! But rather use the *lean* portions and those that will make for body-building forces throughout. Fish and fowl are the preferable meats. No raw meat, and very little ever of hog meat. Only bacon [crisp]. Do not use bacon or fats in cooking the vegetables, for this body; for these tend to add to distresses in those directions of this segregation and breaking of cellular forces throughout the system. 303-11

... keep away from heavy foods. Use those which are body-building, such as beef juices, beef broth, liver, fish, lamb; all may be taken, but never fried foods. 5269-1

It is known that the amino acids in protein are the essential nourishing factor. The flesh itself is not digestible and therefore remains in the system as dross. Perhaps the most important reason for limiting the intake of red meat is that we take on the vibrational pattern of everything we eat. The readings advised against eating pork because it has the lowest vibrational pattern of any meat.

In this world of coffee and carbonated drinks, the drinking of water—*aqua pura*—is not as widely practiced as good health requires.

*(Q) How much water should I drink daily?*

(A) From six to eight tumblers full. 574-1

The readings further stated that foods taken into the body would act in a more beneficial manner if a glass of water was taken before a meal and one just after. The following reading also suggested the drinking of half to three-quarters of a glass of *warm* water immediately upon arising as a way to "clarify the system of poisons."

**. . . for, as has oft been given, when any food value *enters* the stomach *immediately* the stomach becomes a storehouse, or a medicine chest that may create all the elements necessary for proper digestion within the system. If this *first* is acted upon by *aqua pura*, the reactions are more near normal. 311-4**

These dietary suggestions can be habits easily acquired, and once acquired are performed involuntarily, leaving the mind free for greater things.

## Mind Is the Builder

**For in the beginning God moved and mind . . . came into being—and the earth and the fullness thereof became the result of same. 5000-1**

**The mind governs the body more or less; consequently, the mind should dwell on beautiful things if we would have a healthy body. 87-1**

"Mind is the builder." This statement, repeated throughout the readings again and again, is a subject for study in itself. Nobody will doubt the power of the mind, but are we prepared to attribute to it the myriad daily mishaps and unwanted patterns of behavior in our lives? Patterns which *could* be changed by the conscious changing of mental attitudes. Are we prepared to trace many—if not all—of our sickness to attitudes? Should we wish to research this subject, we each have a perfect guinea pig nearer to us than our right hand—ourself.

We can start working on changing some of the more obvious mental patterns first, such as exchanging anger for patience. Anger is itself a sickness of the brain giving rise to many more sicknesses, while patience is something we came into this three-dimensional plane to learn. Patience is not long-suffering, though that is part of the experience too; patience is the joyful acceptance of being. Let us ascertain that our love for those close to us is true love, with no trace of possessive love—this eliminates jealousy. It makes the object of our love feel less like a "thing" and more like a person. Working on these mind twisters individually, one should find one's life changing. Sickness will become less a part of the pattern as harmony enters.

## Eliminations

Seekers after the causes and cures of the many ills which rack the human frame find that the physical readings very often zeroed in on the colon. It has been pinpointed as the hotbed of disease and the breeding ground of microscopic monsters more hideous than have ever been created by the "horror specialists" in Hollywood. However, the elimination of poisons through the alimentary canal is a subject usually discussed between mothers and children under five years of age, after which time it is expected that an entity should be well enough versed in the complicated eliminatory processes of the body to be able to fend for itself. The readings unequivocally state that the body should have at least one complete evacuation each day and if this is not accomplished naturally, we should aid the process.

. . . **there should never be allowed a twenty-four hour period without an evacuation. For this, as indicated, makes for an accumulation of toxic poisons or drosses that tend to make for pressures upon the nervous system, in the sympathetics or the vagus and the cardiac centers, and an engorgement and an enlargement of the heart's activity. Hence the colonic irrigations. Hence the better activities in the food values, rather than such a conglomeration as to make for distressing conditions. Hence, also, the**

constructive mental activities in regard to same.
**294-184**
*(Q) Should anything be taken for eliminations?*
(A) Correct better by the diet than by taking
eliminants, when possible. If not possible to correct
otherwise, take an eliminant, but [alternate] between one time a vegetable laxative and the next
time a mineral eliminant. **3381-1**
*(Q) What laxative is best for this body?*
(A) There should be no one individual laxative.
Rather vary from oils to sodas . . . **294-184**

The use of the enema with a saline solution is perhaps
the easiest method. Other methods include eliminants of
many types: broken doses of olive oil, abdominal mas-
sages with same, castor oil packs and, for almost everybody, an internal wash (colonic) occasionally. The
readings explained that just as we wash the body exter-
nally we should also wash it internally. For this they recommended saline/soda, Glyco-Thymoline, and other
solutions of an alkaline nature, used at body temperature.
They stated that if the specific instructions were followed,
it would be good for the body and would bring a more
natural functioning, strengthening the walls of the colon
and encouraging its muscular activity (peristalsis).

The colon is the main artery of the eliminating system.
If it is obstructed in its function, the other systems of elimination must help to carry the burden. A strong body odor
is evidence of toxins being expelled by the perspiratory
system while halitosis is the result of the respiratory system taking on an extra job. Skin problems are the manifestation of some irregularity in the eliminating processes
and to seek a camouflage for these symptoms will only
*temporarily* disguise the fact that the body's functioning
is off balance. It is unfortunate that people brag that they
"never perspire, even on the hottest days." Perhaps if they
did, their aches and pains would be less apparent. To re-

lease toxins from the system through perspiration is one of nature's ways of cleansing the system and it is frightening to see millions of dollars spent on advertising campaigns that sell products designed to stem this flow.

**. . . those things that have been as a stoppage for the respiratory activity [have] in part affected the *emunctory* circulation, and . . . made the tendency for conditions in the superficial circulation that are unsatisfactory. 563-4**

Deodorant/antiperspirants are available and offered for use not only for the underarm area but also for the groin area. When asked what ingredients in such preparations were harmful, Cayce stated: "Anything that closes the pores of the skin to prevent perspiration." (2072-6)

***(Q) Should one use a deodorant, especially under the arms, to stop perspiration . . . ?***

**(A) The *best* to use—the safest—is soap and water! 404-8**

## Adjustments and Massage

The solutions offered for physical disharmonies were varied. In a survey of the treatments suggested by the readings, mechanical adjustments—through osteopathy and chiropractic—were the most numerous. The correct alignment of the spine allows the body to rally its own healing forces. The readings promised that the body contains within itself all that is necessary for our perfect healing and resuscitation, providing faulty eliminations do not hinder.

**These adjustments are merely to attune the centers of the body with the coordinating forces of [the] cerebrospinal and sympathetic system. Thus the body is purified or attuned so that it in itself and nature does the healing. 3384-2**

**These [osteopathic treatments] are beneficial—**

**whether once a week, once in ten days, twice a month, ten times a year, or forty times a year. When needed, take them! 1710-10**

Massage plays an important part in the coordination of the various tasks that the body has to perform and the oils and combination of oils recommended as the medium include an infinite variety from Russian White Oil to peanut oil.

## Dream Guidance

Where can we turn for guidance? For those of us whose meditations have not yet reached the level of receiving visions, guidance can be sought through dreams, the interpretation of which was given as a most important facet of spiritual growth.

**. . . dreams, in whatever character they may come, are the reflection either of physical condition . . . or of the subconscious, with the conditions relating to the physical body and its action . . . 294-15**

Dreams can give us the answers to questions which are in the foreground of our daily life, despite the fact that they may not have surfaced in the conscious mind. Sometimes we are not ready to accept dream advice, in which case symbols reoccur in various guises until we actually do something about the advice. Anything which might interfere with our harmonious existence rises to the surface of our dreams to be worked out. When we work with our dreams we have an ally which can work with us, side by side, in meeting the opportunities which confront us daily. Dreams may help us make the decisions which will keep us in tune with the world around us. Ignoring our dreams is tantamount to enrolling in college and not attending the lectures. Dream interpretation is an aid which is becoming more widely researched and practiced in the Aquarian Age.

## The Spiritual Path

The readings gave as the basic premise of life that the Lord our God is ONE. Our bodies contain in their three-part unity all that is to be found in the Universe. It is no wonder, then, that every realized man has exhorted us to seek the Truth within ourselves.

This is the spiritual goal achieved by meditation, or seeking to attune ourselves with God. It is the putting aside of our earthly self and practicing the art of "being." Where, then, is one to start? How can one become a part of the Aquarian Age and fit into its pattern, a pattern which is moving toward a world as yet seen only in a dreamlike state? If we are to allow the Cayce readings to guide us, we will begin immediately with that which sings to us the most sweetly. When one piece of the puzzle fits into the picture of life, the movement has been started. Waiting will not make it happen; applying the necessary daily disciplines will. After the first step has been taken, whether in the physical, mental, or spiritual, we are on the path.

# Cooperation and Healing

### by Virginia Fields

To ACHIEVE EFFECTIVE and continuous healing we must search for the cause that has created the mental, physical, spiritual, and emotional imbalance resulting in illness. For at some time, whether in this life or a previous one, disharmony has taken place to the detriment of the physical vehicle. An Edgar Cayce reading defines the basic cause of all illness:

**. . . all illness comes from sin. This everyone must take, whether they like it or not; it comes from sin— whether it be of body, of mind or of soul . . . 3174-1**

We might immediately think of murder, thievery, or assault as being the type of broken commandment that could be termed "sin." However, the Cayce definition of sin engenders a different understanding of the term:

**What is ever the worst fault of each soul?** *Self—self!* **What is the meaning of self? That the hurts, the hindrances are hurts to the self-consciousness; and these create what? Disturbing forces; and these bring about confusions and faults of every nature. For the only sin of man is** *selfishness!* **987-4**

Then, if sin or selfishness is the cause of disease how can we overcome this problem in order to rejuvenate the physical body? The following reading suggested to one person that he seek the *Source* of all healing:

**. . . who healeth all diseases? Uncle John, or God, the Father! This must be determined within self. For, God is spirit and seeketh such to worship Him in spirit and in truth. True, here are pathological conditions that are disturbed with this body. But do the first thing first. There should be a decision within self, first, as to what you believe. And know it must begin with the spiritual purposes of life. 3174-1**

Therefore, if healing comes from attunement with God, why is it that one who is ill finds it difficult at times to reach the "at-onement" that results in healing? Part of the answer is that we can become so enmeshed in the material and physical realities of this plane that the ability to communicate with God is lost. Also, we must take into consideration the misinformation we might have been taught concerning God, disease, and healing. However, no matter what has created the barrier between the individual and God, a higher spiritual understanding must be established to achieve a better balance spiritually, mentally, and physically, in order to have healing. The Cayce readings provide many insights into the attitudes, responsibilities, and applications which can be helpful to those seeking effective and continuous healing.

## Advice for One Seeking Healing

1. We must realize that all healing is from God, and be willing to cooperate with Him to achieve the desired result.

**. . . how well do ye wish to be? How well are ye willing to cooperate, coordinate with the Divine influences which may work in and through thee . . . ? 4021-1**

2. We must wish sincerely to be well and must have an attitude of hopefulness.

**While we have physical conditions that are of the physical-physical, yet the condition through self will gain the greater forces to give the incentives for the physical to become whole, or to function in the normal way. 4208-1**

3. We must gain understanding of the attitudes that create balance and harmony spiritually, mentally, emotionally, and physically.

**. . . the body through its mental forces gains the consciousness of its own condition, and the attributes of the mental with the nerve system, and how this may control the circulation, the assimilation, and those of the system that have to do with the subconscious soul forces of the body . . . 4208-1**

The Cayce literature and tape recordings on healing are excellent sources of material for study to achieve this understanding consciousness. Here are a few examples of the underlying philosophy.

## Spiritual

**Let that mind be in you which was in Jesus . . . 294-71**

## Mental

**Urges arise then, not only from what one eats but from what one thinks; and from what one does about what one thinks and eats! As well as what one digests mentally and spiritually! 2533-6**

## Emotional

**To be sure, attitudes oft influence the physical conditions of the body. No one can hate his neighbor and not have stomach or liver trouble. No one can be jealous and allow the anger of same and not have upset digestion or heart disorder. 4021-1**

**These are a part of the conditions here—animosities, dislikes, jealousies, hates. The expression is first through the sensory organism. Change the body thoughts—we will change the effect upon those activities in the throat, in the eyes, in the ears . . . 3246-2**

The Cayce readings constantly reiterate that we should place our thoughts and emotions in line with the fruits of the spirit as stated in Galatians 5.

## Physical

The suggestions for care of the physical body are encompassed in a variety of Cayce readings on diet and health.

**. . . always will it be found that the *attitude* of the mental forces of a body finds its inception in those things that come into growth; for what we think and what we eat—combined together—*make* what we *are*, physically and mentally. 288-38**

**Here we find the necessity for care, for exercise, for constant checking up on the bodily activities; not daily necessarily—but we remember that the body-**

**physical alters in its expression continually, and by the end of a cycle of seven years it has entirely replaced that which existed at the beginning of the period seven years ago. Replaced with what? The same old tendencies multiplied, the same old inclinations doubled—or eradicated? 2533-6**

4. Since illness begins in selfishness, we *must* learn unselfishness. This can be accomplished by helping other people.

**. . . give of self more to developing of others with its own knowledge as obtained, for this one would well understand that what we give enriches us rather than what we receive, and the account of one's self in every work is the ability to give unto others in this knowledge and understanding . . . Give then the understanding of self, and add to the surrounding forces first that of understanding, of love, of virtue, of knowledge, of faith, of the forces from within, as directed and guided by that ever sourceful force that gives and takes away . . . 4208-1**

5. We must learn to raise within *self* the forces of healing.

**. . . the force within self, through physical rest and the at-oneness with those of the higher forces, attuned with the spirit of self, may work within and give the full understanding of self, and how this self may raise its own forces and not be continually blaming existing conditions upon others . . . 4208-1**

With the seeking of at-onement with God and with balancing of the spiritual, mental, emotional, and physical natures, true and effective healing can begin. However, there is one other factor that must be considered—the channel of healing. Of course, there are times when the seeker can and does reach attunement and healing without the aid of another person; but there are those who for karmic or spiritual reasons need the aid of another. Also, because we are in physical bodies and therefore have learned to rely on our senses, healing in some instances must be aided by things touched, ingested, or seen. Although we may seek spiritually, we may at the same time need therapy understandable to the physical senses such as massage, medication, acupuncture, or osteopathic manipulations, to name only a few. Each person must be aided at the level he can best comprehend, but should seek aid from another only after prayerful meditation.

In seeking a channel of healing, whether from a medical doctor, osteopath, chiropractor, or spiritual healer, one can profit from guidelines in the Cayce readings. Anyone seeking to be a channel of healing should carefully consider the responsibilities, attitudes, and applications as they are presented in the information given for the healing prayer group, which was started in Virginia Beach under the guidance of Edgar Cayce and his readings. The ideals presented in this collection are of great value in understanding the best qualifications that should be found in a healing channel, and to those who desire to prepare themselves so that the power of God can flow through them to others.

## Advice for Channel of Healing

### Responsibilities

1. The ideal must be in Christ.

**In the counsel at the present, then, keep ever before thee thy ideal in the Christ, for the healing, the counsel, the hope, the harmony . . . 281-19**

2. There must be faithfulness to the ideal.

**Be ye then faithful, every one, keeping that counsel, keeping that period of prayer; meeting them that seek in thought and with them present before Him to whom all power is given, that ye all indeed be whole every whit. 281-17**

3. There must be purity of purpose. **Seek experiences not as experiences alone but as purposefulness.** For what be the profit to thyself, to thy neighbor, if experiences alone of such natures rack thy body—owing to its high vibration—without being able to make thee a kinder mother, a more loving wife, a better neighbor, a better individual in every manner? *These* be the fruits, that it makes thee kinder, gentler, stronger in body, in mind, in purpose to be a channel through which the love of *God,* through Jesus Christ, may be manifested in the world. Not as a vision, an experience alone. 281-27

*Attitudes*

1. Love

As ye seek, through raising in self that image of love in Him, so may thine self be lifted up, and the understanding come to him who seeks for same. **281-2**

Be not afraid, ever surrounding self with His presence of love; for He has given His angels charge concerning thee that they bear thee up that thou stumblest not when thou wouldst aid. 281-12

2. Faith

Each seeking for aid may then be aided according to the faith in those that seek to aid in *His* name. **281-2**

3. Sincerity

. . . while all may not wholly understand that which is accomplished through the raising of vibration in self, the directing of vibration to others, these [individuals] may aid with that sincerity that comes with the closer walk with those Creative Forces . . . 281-7

4. Understanding

As ye pray and meditate in Him, so does this arouse or awaken the consciousness in the experience of another that the healing may come; for there must flow out of self Virtue (that is, understanding) for *healing* to be accomplished in another. 281-10

5. Patience

Be not impatient with many who seek and oft appear indigent in their response or activity toward that sought, yet doing all in decency and order. 281-18

Be not fainthearted because, as thou seest, that is not accomplished in a moment. What is eternity to a single experience? "No good shall return to me empty handed." Believest thou? Then thou knowest . . . that as is given out *must* return full measure. 281-4

6. Humility

For, each keeps this ever before self—though chosen as a channel, thou of thyself may do nothing. The Spirit of the Christ, working in and through thee, will bring the fruits of the Spirit in the experience of those that thou would lead to the light. 281-19

7. Cheerfulness

Be cheerful, knowing that as He sees fit, so will He give. Keep on working with, for, toward, the more perfect understanding—each and every one. 281-9

8. Emotional Stability

*(Q) Should one hold a healing meditation for others, when mentally disturbed?*

(A) Oft has it been given as to what may be accomplished. If self is not in an at-onement with the source of power or life or health, best that self in the mental plane set self aright; for, remember, the mental is the builder whether in application of the physical or the spiritual forces. 281-16

*Application*

1. Raising of the Christ vibration.

*(Q) Please give a definition of vibration in relation to healing.*

**(A) This would perhaps require several volumes, to give a complete definition. Vibration is, in its simple essence or word, raising the Christ Consciousness in self to such an extent as it may flow out of self to him thou would direct it to . . . What flowed out of Peter or John? That as received by knowing self in its entirety, body, mind, soul, is one with that Creative Energy that is Life itself! 281-7**

2. Raising of the healing vibration.

*(Q) Should all treatments be made with or through one of the three, three-dimensional vibrations?*

**(A) Either through the one or the three, dependent . . . as to the consciousness necessary to be raised in the individual that seeks; for He took individuals *where* they were, in their own environ, their own surroundings, and transmitted to their consciousness—either by act, word or deed—that necessary to awaken or allow that necessary to bring healing to those who sought for same. 281-12**

These steps can be accomplished through prayer, meditation, and counseling and by keeping self pure in purpose and in attunement with the Source. The next steps are directed chiefly to those who seek to heal through prayer and the laying on of hands.

3. Transferral of the vibration within the healer to the patient.

**Pray [often], and see those forces that would hinder—when the body would in itself have that about self that would eliminate those disturbing factors—*seeing* her, herself, her inner self, *conquering* those forces through Him. 281-7**

a. Transfer vibration by thought.

*(Q) How can one direct the vibration . . . ?*

**(A) By thought. (Now we are speaking of a purely mechanical, metaphysical-spiritual activity which**

**would take place.) One has directed their thought to an individual who is to** *receive* **the blessing of that power or force raised. They raise within themselves that which may be sent out as a power, and it passes to those that would be in attune or accord. Were they present, a much greater force may be felt, to be sure; less in the strain upon the physical body. 281-14**

b. Transfer the vibration by word when possible.

**. . . to the more individuals it is true that the spoken word makes a higher vibration. 281-9**

c. Transfer the vibration by the laying on of hands when led to do so.

**The manner of overcoming [ills], as has been intimated, may best be accomplished with the laying on of hands, that enables . . . the entity so being aided to have** *something* **to hold on to that is as concrete as that [illness] it is battling with . . .**

**As the body attunes self, as has been given, it may be a channel where there may be even** *instant* **healing with the laying on of hands. The more often this occurs, the more** *power* **is there felt in the body, the more forcefulness in the act or word. 281-5**

When the concepts given in the readings are applied, healing may be more rapidly and effectively achieved; herein can be learned the valuable lesson of loving cooperation which is grace in action. *A Search for God, Book I,* reminds us: "As we seek, in our way, to cooperate in being of service to others, we are lifted up. Let us, then, express the Creative Force within us in such a way that it may bring hope, peace and understanding into the lives of others, that they too, in their way, may seek to be channels of blessings."

By learning cooperation, the one who is healed can be of service to others, and thus the cycle of brother aiding brother grows and spreads as the circles that enlarge and grow when a pebble is dropped in a quiet pool. Thus comes the realization that in being a blessing to others we "become conscious that our lives are spent in the way He would have us go, and that His presence abides with us" *(Search for God, Book I)*, and that through loving service to others and the consciousness of God's presence within, effective and continuous healing of spirit, mind, and body is achieved.

# Cycle of Consciousness:
## Life and Death
◆
### by Margaret Ray

LIFE. DEATH. BY their inevitability, these two experiences lie at the root of man's consciousness, tantalizing him with the elusiveness of accurate definition, creating within him a vague anxiety.

It is just this universality of experience, just this absence of shared understanding which precipitates the extremes of man's attitudes toward them. By limited definition, life and death are opposites—each condition characterized by the absence of the other—their opposing descriptive qualities varied only by the terminology of the observer, compatible with his specific field of interest. For the biologist, life involves movement, reproduction, self-preservation. To the chemist it manifests as elements in combination with carbon. To those without enthusiasm for scientific research and to those unable or unwilling to discern the inner anxiety, both life and death simply are— to be enjoyed or endured as the case may be.

Regardless of one's point of view, however, the two conditions must be dealt with by everyone, a fact sufficient in itself to compel investigation by those whose interest lies always in uncovering truth. It is for such persons that a more definitive understanding of both life and death becomes imperative. It is for them that the information in the Edgar Cayce readings assumes such significance, and the Library Series book, *On Life and Death*, affords a wealth of psychic material which can hardly fail to excite the inquiring mind.

With or without metaphysical delving, man finds himself hard put to verbalize with certainty whether his time on earth is spent in living or in dying. To even the casual observer, either statement contains truth. Is it not possible—probable, even—that there is a similar paradox in what he calls death? Just as man sees himself as "living" or "dying," the difference existing only in the direction of his attention, is it not likely that so-called death is also an attention-directing situation? But what of this "attention"? It can only be of consciousness, and it is this consciousness which is, according to the readings, man's essence, his reality.

If, then, man comes to see that consciousness is the surest definition of himself, he will begin to search for all its dimensions. He will ponder the nature of that consciousness in normal waking states, in his dreams, under the influence of anesthetics or other drugs, under conditions of trauma, and all other situations. It will then probably seem reasonable that his consciousness in "death"—just as in these life states is no more than a movement, a redirecting of attention. Death will then be merely a leaving off of one set of awarenesses for the adoption of another.

Such an understanding of the life-death relationship

would more nearly satisfy man's consummate desire for infinite existence. He would be less apprehensive about his seemingly inevitable physical demise. The energies previously invested in this apprehension would then be available for discovering and fulfilling the purpose of his having been born.

Man's evolvement of that understanding—his demonstration of it—is his only reason for being, according to the Cayce readings. The following extracts, gleaned from *On Life and Death,* are illustrative of such a conclusion:

**For there is no death when the entity or the real self is considered; only the change in the consciousness of being able to make application in the sphere of activity in which the entity finds self. 2147-1**

**Yet if we learn more and more that separations are only walking through the rooms as it were of God's house, we become—in these separations, in these experiences—aware of what is meant by that which has been and is the law, as from the beginning; "Know, O ye peoples, the Lord thy God is one!"**

**And ye must be one—one with another, one with Him—if ye would be, as indeed ye are, corpuscles in the *life flow* of thy Redeemer! 1391-1**

**The earth's sojourns also make for such close associations with why the entity from one realm of experience to another experiences the entering of those realms from the application of the entity, as we have indicated, in each earthly realm.**

**Then, a death in the flesh is a birth into the realm of another experience, to those who have lived in such a manner as not to be bound by earthly ties. This does not mean that it does not have its own experience about the earth, but that it has lived such a *fullness* of life that it must be about its business. 989-2**

It appears that man's presence on the earth is no accident. His reasons for being born, according to the readings, are very specific. He is here for experiences which are "stepping-stones to the greater consciousness," here to demonstrate what he has been learning about himself through the ages. The truth he must learn is that we all are one. We have not really learned that truth, however, until our actions *show* it. The earth is a proving ground—a place for examinations and a time for us to use physical bodies for demonstrating the understanding we have gained.

**Know that it is not all just to live—not all just to be good, but good for something; that ye may fulfill that purpose for which ye have entered this experience.**

**And that purpose is that you might know yourself to be yourself, and yet one with the Creative Forces, or God. 2030-1**

**For, remember, it is not all of life just to live nor yet all of death to die. For it is self that one has to meet. And what ye sow—mentally, spiritually, physically—that ye *will* eventually reap. And the laborer is worthy of his hire; or that effort, that purpose for which ye as an entity plan, consider, has already brought in eternity its own shadow of things to be. 257-249**

Once man understands that he is but part of a Whole, that he is separated from its other parts only by his own consciousness, his preoccupation with his physical body gives way to a growing interest in his mental and spiritual "bodies." He then seeks to define all of these three aspects of himself and to bring them into harmony. The Cayce readings say plainly that man is a physical-mental-spiritual entity and they stress the importance of a well-rounded life in which all three parts of this trinity will be fully developed. It is a familiar concept, but one to which the readings add unfamiliar dimensions.

**But keep *balanced*—keep coordinated. Know that**

there are material laws, there are mental laws, there are spiritual laws. And just as it is necessary for the body to coordinate—mentally, physically and spiritually—so must the rules or the laws coordinate and cooperate.

Then study to show thyself approved a workman not ashamed; rightly dividing the words of truth, keeping self unspotted from the world—or from questionings of thine own conscience. And ye will find ye will go a long way, finding harmony and happiness as ye create and bring it about in the bodily activities of others. 1670-1

Each entity is a part of the universal whole. All knowledge, all understanding that has been a part of the entity's consciousness, then, is a part of the entity's experience.

Thus the unfoldment in the present is merely becoming aware of that experience through which the entity—either in body or in mind—has passed in a consciousness.

Hence there are two phases, or two means of expression from which urges arise in the experience of the entity. There is the form of consciousness attained when absent from the body, whether in normal sleep or in that sleep called death (in the earth plane). Then there is the consciousness to the soul-entity.

For, the entity finds itself body-physical, body-mind, body-soul. The body-soul is a citizen of that realm we call heaven, as much as the body-physical is a citizen of the land we call home.

These are the forms or the premises, then, through which influences arise. 2823-1

In the development of these three aspects of himself, it is necessary that man come to the realization that they are interdependent. Unquestionably, he will make this discovery. The readings have much to say about this interaction and man's realization of it as he seeks harmony within himself.

**Do not starve either of these phases of thy unfoldment, for all that is in mind and body first appears in spirit.** Keep each, then, in its proper relation one to another, if the entity would contribute the more to the activities in the earth . . . In applying self, know thy own weaknesses, as well as thy own virtues. Set them down in a row, not in the same row; but every few weeks rub out those that you have overcome or add those that you know you have taken on. This will help you keep that balance that is so unusual in the entity. 3652-1

Well, too, that the body take some *definite* exercise in the *open.* This should be to keep the mental and the physical well-balanced together.

In the spiritual life, keep close to that as has been accorded in the mental forces of the body—knowing that in the understanding of the relationships of the spiritual body there must be need of the mental and physical for its material manifestation . . . whatever there may be conceived by the mind of a body, it finds *its* replica in a material experience; for with the body, mind and spirit does one present itself *wholly* acceptable *unto* the divine, *whatever* that may be made in the terms of worshipfulness; for *in* the spiritual one lives, moves, and has one's being—and the spirit is willing, and the flesh will follow, will the mental build in that direction that they are *kept* in accord one with another. 454-1

With the expansion of his consciousness, man's concept of purpose undergoes a change. In addition, the enlargement of his understanding of the reality of himself results in his increasing ability to discipline himself. He increasingly makes use of his will. He must *will* to give each aspect of himself its proper care. His time must be con-

sciously budgeted so that all elements of his life will receive the attention they require for perfect functioning.
Further, he discovers that the needs he had known in his
physical body—food, elimination, exercise, relaxation—
have their counterparts in the mental and the spiritual. The
readings make it clear that such is the case.

**First making for self in all of its activities, certain
periods for rest, for mental exertion, for mental activity, periods of recreation in the various characters and natures; in other words, budgeting the time,
and yet making for advancement not as rote or as
just plain routine but see the value in self, in self's
development, of so budgeting self and self's activities as to know that the best or the better balance
may be kept within self in its advancement in every
phase of its mental, physical or spiritual activity. Do
not neglect one for another, but to be well-balanced
is only to be well-equipped and doesn't mean movement or activity has begun. The knowledge of self,
the knowledge of the various influences in the experience of self is only valuable or constructive when
applied in the experience of self. Hence, get busy!
440-11**

**So, in the diets, in the activities, do those things
that bring harmony, peace in the body.**

**When there are those desires or cravings, do not
give way but don't deny those things, for there are
those elements within same where there are the demands for that necessary for creating the balance
within the system. For it has been given oft, there is
in a normal healthy individual (alive)** *every element*
**that is known—or may be known—outside of that
body! Hence for these to live in harmony it becomes
necessary that an even balance be kept within and
without. Just as when there are the atmospheric
pressures upon a body, the body finds itself adjust-**

ing itself to the various changes. Whether the barometer is high or low, the body—while feeling the effect, unless there be a deficiency in the activity of some organ—in a moment *adjusts* itself to same! And this should be the same activity throughout the diets of a body. He that sets a rule must live and die by the rule! But he that makes the rule may use and apply those things within and without in such measures, such ways and manners, that will make for the creating of coordination.

Do not be excessive in anything! Do not be *abnormal! Let's be normal in everything.* 340-29

As man consistently endeavors to love and care for each part of himself, as he becomes more and more aware of the interaction of all facets of his existence, and as he strives to bring them into perfect balance, his awareness of similar relationships in the universe is sharpened. He becomes more conscious of his own position in a universal harmony. His purpose becomes that of self-attunement to universal laws, realizing that every experience is an opportunity for him to exercise his understanding of those laws. Little by little he understands that the unity he has begun to realize within himself is a miniature of an infinite universal unity. He begins to experience the Law of Love.

. . . know that all life is one before Him (or all lives, if ye choose to term it so), even as thy Lord, thy God is one.

Thus each experience builds the ability of the individual, either mentally, spiritually or physically, to make application in whatever may be the next experience.

And in this relationship, remember that opportunity arises with each meeting, each association. Each problem has its opportunity for choice of spiritual, mental, material opportunities. They are one in their greater, their better sense. 2489-1

An experience, then, is not only a happening, but what is the reaction in your own mind? What does it do to you to make your life, your habits, your relationships to others of a more helpful nature, with a more hopeful attitude?

These are the criterions for every individual's experience—sincerity of purpose, of desire; putting the whole law into effect in the activities—which is to love the Lord thy God with all thy heart, thy mind, thy body, and thy neighbor as thyself.

This is the whole law. All the other things given or written are only the interpreting of same . . .

And we choose each day *whom* we will serve! And by the records in time and space, as we have moved through the realms of His kingdom, we have left our mark upon same. 1567-2

Coming more and more to understand himself, his purpose, his relationship to universal forces, man gradually ceases to attach the blame for his difficulties on external influences, either persons or material conditions. He becomes responsible for himself, realizing that his own choices have attracted them all. The truth that one can reap only what one has sown becomes real truth for him, and his inner demand that he project only love and good will becomes increasingly urgent. As he practices such responsibility, consistently observing his true purpose and making repeated choices which are consistent with that purpose, he knowingly, consciously, prepares his soul for its intended place in the universal harmony. The refining of this attitude requires unlimited patience.

For man and woman in their manifestation are given—by the All-Wise, All-Merciful Father, the First Cause, the Mother-God, the Father-God—the opportunity to be one with Him. Hence they are given the attributes of the various phases through which the entity or soul may become conscious or aware of that

Presence abiding with or withdrawing from its activities; dependent, to be sure, upon how that entity or soul uses the opportunities.

For without the gift of free will to the soul, how could it become aware of the Presence of the All-Abiding Creative Force or Energy called God? 945-1

Let the law of the *Lord,* as *thou knowest* it in thine heart, *be* the *rule* of *thy* life—and thy dealings with thy fellowman! And ye will find that the growth of the mind-spiritual, of the mind-mental, of the body-physical, will open the way for thee, day by day.

For, as those laws that become as but watchwords to many on the tower, there is a whole day's work before thee each day, with all its glorious opportunities of seeing the glory of the Lord manifested by thine own acts!

Yet if that which confronts thee makes for discouragement, harshness of words, lack of enthusiasm, or those things that make for doubts or fears, the opportunity has turned its back—and what *is* the outlook? Doubt and fear!

Study, then, to show thyself approved, *each day!* *Do what* thou *knowest* to do, to be aright! Then *leave* it *alone!* God giveth the *increase! Thy* worry, *thy* anxiety, only will produce disorder in *thine* own mind!

For the application in self, the *try,* the effort, the energy expended in the proper direction, is all that is required of *thee.* God giveth the increase. 601-11

Throughout his lifetime man's chief business, it would seem, is to find out who and what he really is. Succinctly phrased, he develops consciousness. It is this consciousness, according to the readings, which has infinite potential capacity for expansion, is the real self which intuitively seeks eternal existence. Unrestricted by the physical laws governing the earth and its environs, this consciousness—

ill-defined in physical terms—is at liberty to escape earth's gravitational pull and visits other planes within the universe, unimpeded by time and space.

The Cayce materials make this superior, non-earthbound consciousness entirely credible. It is that part of man which transcends all physical limitations and in doing so makes of life and death a continuing experience. In the earth plane man uses his physically oriented mind as a receptor for messages originating in this superconsciousness, this mind operating according to man's selective will. In other realms of universal consciousness, this physical mind is absent, the consciousness pursuing its purpose at the direction of a more primary force, Spirit. It is necessary for the consciousness to find itself under both kinds of influences for its total understanding of itself, and accounts for the cyclic repetition of "births" and "deaths." According to the readings, death—like birth—is merely a transition, a passing through "God's other door," a passing from one plane of consciousness to another.

In this way, over eons of varied experiences, the soul comes to the ultimate truth that all is One. It "knows itself to be itself yet one with the Whole." At last omnipresent, omniscient, it is also omnipotent—in complete harmony with, one with, the Universal Creative Forces which, the readings say, "man calls God."

# The Significance of Atlantis for Our Time

## by Harvey Humann

IT IS NOT my purpose here to prove Atlantis but rather to point to a few clues indicative of its existence and, of more importance, to describe its significance for our time. It is not surprising that this ancient story about the lost continent of Atlantis, with its alleged brilliance, intrigues us today even as it did the Athenians when Plato first told it to them some 2,500 years ago. It has all the makings of great mythology. It reaches back to a dim past with a cast of gods, god-kings, and priests, power, riches, a strong dash of the supernatural, and, finally, a sudden and catastrophic end as it sank into the sea.

The Atlantis story describes a super civilization and a culture that far outstrips the twentieth century in its advanced technology, its science, mathematics, and astronomy. In fact, the Atlantean accomplishments seem to rival those in modern science fiction. For thousands of years, in scores of countries around the world, the story has persisted.

The oldest recorded version of the Atlantis story comes from Plato's "Critias," but it is in his dialogue "Timaeus" that he reveals the source of his story. Plato says that Solon, the great Athenian statesman, spent ten years in Egypt with the priests in the temples of Sais, a city at the head of the Egyptian Delta. The priests contended that the temples contained the records of events of great antiquity. There, Plato reports, Solon heard the details of this ancient and unusual civilization. Atlantis, they said, was a great continent "situated to the West of the straits called Hercules."

Its rulers, Plato goes on to say, were powerful, all-wise god-kings and priests who were direct descendants of the gods. Their superior wisdom enabled them to develop a culture that has never been equaled. The god-like nature of the Atlanteans lasted for many, many years. Then, he says, something happened—" . . . this divine portion began to fade away in them, and became diluted too often and with too much of the mortal admixture, and the human nature got the upper hand; then they, being unable to bear their fortune, became unseemly . . . they began to appear base . . . they were filled with unrighteousness, avarice and power." Because of their growing intolerable wickedness the gods brought about their downfall (" . . . there occurred violent earthquakes and floods; and in a single day and night of rain . . . Atlantis disappeared . . . and was sunk beneath the sea"). Plato gives the date of this catastrophe as 9,000 years before his time.

H.G. Wells, who certainly knows his tales and myths, says of Atlantis: "There is a magic in names . . . and the mightiest among these words of magic is Atlantis . . . It is as if this vision of a lost culture touched the most hidden part of the soul."

In D.H. Lawrence's book, *Fantasia of the Unconscious*, the magic name of Atlantis appears. Lawrence says, "I honestly think that the great pagan world of which Egypt and Greece were the last living terms . . . once had a vast and perhaps a perfect science, a science in terms of life. I believe it was esoteric, invested in a large priesthood . . . taught esoterically in all countries of the globe, Asia, Polynesia, Atlantis, and Europe . . . Man wandered back and forth from Atlantis to Polynesia as men now sail from Europe to America."

Historian Ernest Renan claims there is wide evidence that Egypt sprang full blown as a sophisticated civilization. He contends that Egyptian mathematics, architecture, and science seem to have appeared suddenly. Egypt, he says, seems never to have had a stage of barbarism or primitivism but seems to have occurred instantly as a mature civilization.

One of the basic reasons Atlantis intrigues us as possible history is simply that scientists and historians really do not know the beginnings of man. They do not know where man first lived or from where he came. They do not know the time of appearance nor the origin of the five races. Anthropologists cannot tell us with real authority the time nor place of the oldest civilization. Furthermore, they cannot explain the origin of scores of artifacts found in many parts of the world that point to some brilliant ancient achievements. The conjectures and theories about prehistory are oftentimes simple hypotheses and over-generalizations based on mere fragments of evidence.

Richard Leakey, the eminent anthropologist, in reporting a find of a fragmented skull of early man near Lake Rudolph, Kenya, pushed the beginnings of man back over a million years. Leakey said the skull he found was 2.5 million years old or 1.5 million years older than any previous evidence of man. It is obvious that there are still million-year gaps in our knowledge of pre-history. It is the persistence of hundreds of unanswered questions about the origin of early cultures that keeps the legend of Atlantis alive.

Recorded history is, admittedly, a rather poor guide into the ancient past. Nineteenth-century historians never suspected that beneath the Babylonian empire there existed an even older civilization of Sumerians, and Sumerian mythology tells about an earlier culture, that of Atlantis.

From widely separated traditions of the world come countless versions of stories, rites, myths, and words that point to a common origin. Deluge stories appear in the literature of scores of countries, including the legends of the American Mandan Indians and a tribe of Amazon natives. Stories coming from such widespread and diverse cultures could not possibly have all been merely products of creative imaginations. It seems more likely that such stories must first have come from some remembrance of a real and terrible event. If the Atlanteans migrated and colonized many parts of the world, they might well have been the source of these flood stories.

For thousands of years Homer's stories of Troy were considered pure fable, yet archaeologist Heinrich Schliemann found Troy just where Homer had said it was. For centuries there were myths and fables about a buried city called Pompeii. These stories were always referred to as fables, yet when Pompeii was uncovered, it was found to be just as the fables had described it. Here, actual history—as recent as 70 A.D., when the city was buried by volcanic action—became a myth, and only the legend of Pompeii kept the history of that city alive.

There are, in fact, a number of esoteric teachers who maintain that in many instances truth is more faithfully transmitted from age to age through myths and symbols than through written history.

The existence of Atlantis as the possible mother of all civilizations would completely rewrite the history we accept today and provide the key piece to a massive jigsaw puzzle that scientists and anthropologists have been trying to piece together for centuries.

The nearly 700 Edgar Cayce readings that refer to Atlantis have not only rekindled interest in the story of the lost continent, but also these readings have stressed a great spiritual significance that is specifically relevant to our century.

The readings amplify the Plato story. Whereas Plato tells about a single great catastrophe, the readings say Atlantis was destroyed in three, distinctly separate, cataclysmic actions. The first disturbance came before 50,000 B.C. The second inundation came about 28,000 B.C. and left that continent divided into three rather large islands. The third and final catastrophe came in 10,700 B.C.

The readings report that before and after each of these disturbances there were sizable dispersions of Atlanteans into Peru, Yucatan, Central America, Egypt, and many other lands. These migrating Atlanteans were the scientists, teachers, priests, and craftsmen that moved each country they touched into accelerated development. The readings say that Atlantis reached a level of spiritual and material greatness that has never been equaled. The great tragedy, the readings point out, is that the vast knowledge of universal laws which so dramatically enhanced this culture's technology was also the cause of its destruction. The readings also indicate that many souls on earth today have had a previous incarnation on Atlantis. Their talents, wisdom, and scientific contributions, stored in the unconscious mind, are manifesting themselves again today.

**For, it is not by chance that any soul enters a particular period. As indicated in this entity here, it is an Atlantean. Hence it is manifesting in the earth at a period when many Atlanteans have entered. For, ye may be very sure there is not a leader in any country or any clime, whether friend or foe of what this**

**entity thinks, that was not an Atlantean. 2794-3**

We are moving into an era when our concepts of improvement in terms of instruments, machines, and technical processes are changing to newer concepts of inner improvement and understanding. An awareness of new priorities is emerging through the reappearance everywhere of large numbers of action-oriented Atlanteans, who are stirring things up with aggressiveness.

There is an intriguing reading about the possible influence Atlantean souls "on the other side" may be exerting on fellow Atlanteans already in the earth plane, "either through the direct influence of being regenerated, or reincarnated into the earth, or through that of the mental application [or] through the influences as may be had upon thought of individuals or groups by speaking from that environ." (364-3)

Another reading says that "the Atlanteans are all *exceptional*. They either wield woe or great development. And their influences are felt, whether the individual recognizes it in himself or not." (1744-1)

It is, perhaps, for this reason that some former Atlanteans are drawing attention to age-old values and ideals with a kind of militant urgency. Their presence is being felt most effectively in areas of social justice and world brotherhood. This age, the readings say, is providing them their first opportunity to meet themselves again under Atlantean conditions in order to make amends for their former failures.

All of this, however, is not going on without a struggle. The powerful forces of Belial, the ancient materialists who first precipitated the Atlantis catastrophe, are still strongly entrenched. This is a rematch between the two powerful forces. It is a moral and spiritual struggle.

**The Sons of Belial were of one group, or those that sought more the gratifying, the satisfying, the use of material things for self, *without* thought or consideration as to the sources of such nor the hardships**

in the experiences of others. Or, in other words, as we would term it today, they were those without a standard of morality.

The other group—those who followed the Law of One—had a standard. The Sons of Belial had no standard, save of self, self-aggrandizement. 877-26

. . . the entity was in the Atlantean land, during the period just before the breaking up of the land in the second period of its destruction.

The entity was among the children of the Law of One . . . [and] made for those activities in which there were the periods brought when the Sons of Belial besought the daughters of the children of the Law of One. The encouragements made for that period of rebellion in which there was the using of spiritual forces as a destructive influence to material things. 2594-1

The Atlanteans had a profound knowledge of spiritual and natural laws which are basically interrelated. They studied and used the vibration of plants, jewels, metals, and many other creative energies of the universe. They knew the secret of neutralizing the pull of gravity which permitted the lifting of great stones in the building of temples and pyramids.

. . . that ability lying within each to be transposed in thought as in body . . . not only able to build that as able to transpose or build up the elements about them but to transpose them bodily from one portion of the universe to the other, through the uses of not only those recently rediscovered gases, and those of the electrical and aeriatic formations in the breaking up of the atomic forces to produce impelling force to those means and modes of transposition, or of travel, or of lifting large weights, or of changing the faces or forces of nature itself . . . 364-4

. . . the entity was in the Atlantean land when

**there were the preparations of those things that had pertained to the ability for the application of appliances to the various elements known as electrical forces in the present day; as to the manners and ways in which the various crafts carried individuals from place to place, and what may be known in the present as the photographing from a distance, or the fields of activity that showed the ability for reading inscriptions through walls—even at distances, or for the preparations of the elevations in the various activities where there was the overcoming of (termed today) the forces of nature or gravity itself; and the preparations through the crystal, the mighty, terrible crystal . . . 519-1**

The readings suggest that mental telepathy was a natural mode of communication in Atlantis. They mention aircraft, submarines, atomic energy, and lasers as commonplace in its technology. But the great firestone that gathered cosmic and solar energy for many uses was perhaps the most fascinating and complex of all the technical advances discussed in the readings. It is significant that this great firestone was designed and built by the spiritual initiates of Atlantis. It was at first in their custody. Only they understood the spiritual and natural laws that manifested through this great crystal.

**The preparation of this stone was in the hands only of the initiates at the time, and the entity was among those that directed the influences of the radiation that arose in the form of the rays that were invisible to the eye but that acted upon the stones themselves as set in the motivating forces—whether the aircraft that were lifted by the gases in the period or whether guiding the more pleasure vehicles that might pass along close to the earth, or what would be termed the crafts on the water or under the water. 440-5**

The secret of this fantastic crystal is still preserved. When the Sons of the Law of One left Atlantis because they had been forewarned about the coming catastrophe, they took with them the secret records of this exotic device. They also took records of their history, their religion, and their scientific achievements. According to the readings, these records are quite definitive and, when found, will reveal:

**A record of Atlantis from the beginnings of those periods when the Spirit took form or began the encasements in that land, and the developments of the peoples throughout their sojourn, with the record of the first destruction and the changes that took place in the land, with the record of the *sojournings* of the peoples to the varied activities in other lands, and a record of the meetings of all the nations or lands for the activities in the destructions that became necessary with the final destruction of Atlantis and the building of the pyramid of initiation, with who, what, where, would come the opening of the records that are as copies from the sunken Atlantis; for with the change it must rise (the temple) again . . . [The records are] to be opened only when there was the returning of those into materiality, or to earth's experience, when the change was imminent in the earth; which change, we see, begins in '58 and ends with the changes wrought in the upheavals and the shifting of the poles, as begins then the reign in '98 (as time is counted in the present) of those influences that have been given by many in the records that have been kept. 378-16**

The records will not just be opened by chance.

**. . . as time draws nigh when changes are to come about, there may be the opening of those three places [Egypt, Yucatan, and Atlantis] where the records are one, to those that are the initiates in the knowledge of the One God. 5750-1**

These records will unlock scientific and spiritual secrets, and with these disclosures will come difficult options and tests—whether to use this knowledge for good or for evil.

One reading told a woman that she failed in her last opportunity.

**This, then, is the purpose of the entity in the earth: To be a channel of blessing to someone today, now; to be a living example of that He gave, "Come unto me, all that are weak and heavy laden—take my Cross upon you and learn of me."**

**These are thy purposes in the earth. These ye will manifest beautifully or make a miserable failure again—as ye did in Atlantis, as many another soul in this particular era is doing.**

**Which will it be? 2794-3**

What then is the central significance of Atlantis for our time? Atlantis stands as an awesome example of spiritual failure of a great civilization. We are again being asked to choose whom we would serve. If we choose wrongly again, as many of us did before, we might possibly wait many lifetimes for the same opportunities we have today.

We sometimes think we need to make only one great decision in choosing whom we would serve. Unfortunately, this is not so, We need constantly to make decisions that will keep us on the spiritual path. It is not usually anything dramatic but rather a slow and steady growth toward spiritual ideals. We need constantly to remind ourselves why we are here so that we may fulfill, in the earth, the purpose for which we came into being—now. The principles and ideals for our sojourn here on earth have not changed through eons of time. But we sometimes become insensitive and indifferent to these principles. This was the tragedy of Atlantis.

Most of us know what we need to do to stay on the spiritual path. Our awareness, however, is sometimes unresponsive to our ideals. We need to practice those activities that will sharpen our awareness so that what we do is never far removed from what we know we should do. In other words, we need to apply—to live—what we believe.

# What Is Patience?

by The Reverend Ernestine G. Busch

THERE ARE NUMEROUS references in the Edgar Cayce readings concerning time, space, and patience. While these references are an attempt to communicate infinite concepts to the finite mind, it is sometimes difficult for that limited mind to adapt itself to such limitless dimensions and to understand clearly what the words mean.

**In man's consciousness there appears so much mercy, so much love, that these have been called time and space. 3660-1**

Where does this leave patience? We think we know the word. We think we understand it. Is there more to it than appears to our conscious minds? Perhaps there is. Let us consider some possibilities:

**The records are upon time and space, which are**

**manifestations of that influence or force we call God. They are both old and ever new. But only in patience does the finite mind become aware of the *value* of same upon the infinite, or the spiritual self. 2144-1**

The possibility that patience might be truth suggests itself, but we find:

*Truth* **is as experience. Hence** *is* **an earning, through the manners in which a finite mind becomes conscious of what Truth is. Hence Truth is a growth, and hence an** *earning,* **a yearning, a growing, and is** *earned* **by he or she that applies that known in the manner that** *is* **in keeping with His Will, rather than that there may be the satisfying of self's own desires . . . Truth is as that which may be earned through the** *experiencing* **of the knowledge and understanding concerning the laws of truth . . . 262-19**

Bible definitions of truth are "thy law is the truth" (Ps. 119:142), "all thy commandments are truth" (Ps. 119:151), and "thy word is truth." (John 17:17) Dictionary definitions of truth are: reality, veracity, fact, and righteousness.

Patience is defined in the dictionary as: suffering with calmness, persevering, calmly enduring, long-suffering. In the Bible, Revelation 13:10 gives a definition of sorts, "He that leadeth into captivity shall go into captivity: he that killeth with the sword must be killed with the sword. Here is the patience and the faith of the saints." Hebrews 12:1 advises, "let us with patience run the race that is set before us."

So patience is not truth. Yet, the feeling persists that patience has something to do with truth. Matthew 18:21-35 gives an example of patience in forgiveness, not just seven times seven but seventy times seven. Perhaps patience has to do with the application of truth.

**Beautiful truths without personal application by the one presenting them is indeed casting pearls to swine . . . 262-13**

Reading 3051-7 gives the cause of impatience as "neglecting to keep the law." Since "thy law is the truth," let us consider the possibilities in thinking of patience as being the application of truth. Perhaps, before we can understand the foreverness of God's mercy or the fullness of His love, we must experience the dispassion of His truth by applying the law of love in everyday living, to enemies and friends alike.

In such a case, patience should be organized and related to one's "work" or "race" (contest), yet oriented both to God and to man. Problems must be seen clearly and met, not hastily, but as one trying to do or say the right thing, at the right time, in the right way.

Patience, then, does not consist solely of suffering in silence. There may be activity, but the activity must be of a certain kind:

**. . . just be patient with self and with others. The more patience that is shown in self toward others, the more patience will be shown by others to self— and it becomes then a circle, as it were . . . Being patient, then, with self first, being patient then with others. As the patience is manifest, so will the results be seen. This doesn't mean patience in the sense of just submissiveness, or just being quiet— but an *active* patience, *conscious* of being patient with self and with others. 911-3**

Yet there are times when it is necessary to suffer in silence:

**It is best to be patient and quiet than to be sorry. For, remorse or regret causes a great deal of self-condemnation, and this no entity should do. 3135-1**

Some may find it difficult to think of patience as being the application of truth. Luke 21:19 is frequently quoted in the readings. "In your patience possess ye your souls." (KJV) The newest expanded translation of the New Testament expresses this verse, "In the sphere of your steadfastness, constancy, and endurance you shall win for your-selves your lives." Yet steadfastness, constancy, and en-durance must be applied in some practical way:

**. . . know that the truth is applicable in every ex-perience of the entity's life, whether as a shoestring vendor or . . . a director of some great financial insti-tution, or even a leader or ruler over many peoples. 3063-1**

**Thus the pattern, the book of life is written by the entity in its use of truth, knowledge, wisdom, in its dealings with its fellowman through the material so-journs. 2620-2**

Truth is never doormat material. While one must accept what cannot be changed so long as it cannot be changed in the present, this should not prevent one from being alert to the possibility of change in the future:

**To be sure, patience, long-suffering and endurance are in their respective manners urges that would lead to virtues, but they cease to be a virtue when the individual entity allows self merely to be im-posed upon, and to take second place merely because someone else, of a more aggressive nature, imposes. 3029-1**

It is interesting to note that in different readings pa-tience is related to the Holy Spirit. The Holy Spirit is pic-tured in the Bible as the author of the new birth, the source of wisdom, the source of miraculous power, the witness; inspiring scripture, appointing ministers, directing where the Gospel was not to be preached, in-dwelling saints, sanctifying the church; striving with sinners, creating and giving life, commissioning servants, teaching, helping our infirmities, searching all things, working according to His own will, speaking in and by the prophets; as the Com-forter, edifying the church, imparting the love of God, com-municating joy, and imparting hope.

The fruit of the Spirit is presented in Galatians 5:22-23

as "love, joy, peace, long-suffering, gentleness, goodness, faith, meekness, temperance." Ephesians 5:9 gives the fruit of the Spirit as being "in all goodness and righteousness and truth."

Less familiar to many are the gifts of the Spirit set forth in I Corinthians 12:8-10, but for a complete understanding it is best to read all of Chapters 12 and 13, and through 14:33, for much is found concerning the use of the gifts of the Spirit which is easily overlooked, neglected, or misunderstood. Briefly, the gifts of the spirit are given as: the word of wisdom, the word of knowledge, faith, healing, the working of miracles, prophecy, discerning of speaking in tongues, and interpreting tongues.

If patience can indeed work so greatly in us, it would seem to be well worth our while to cultivate it. Perhaps the answer as to how patience might be able to work so greatly in us is found in this reading where it is described as a unifying force:

**For to the entity—as to the world—patience is the lesson that each soul must learn in its sojourn through materiality. And this is a thought for the entity: Time, space and patience are in the mental realm the same as implied by the expression "Father-God, Son and Holy Spirit," or as Spirit, Body, Soul. They are expressions of the three-dimensional thought.**

**And in patience, then does man become more and more aware *of* the continuity of life of his soul being a portion of the Whole; Patience being the portion of man's sphere of activity in the finite being, as Time and Space manifest the creative and motivative force . . . patience will bring the full union of time and space that encompasses that honor, that knowledge which the entity has had and which is so innate, and that may be expressed in, *"Know, O peoples, the Lord thy God is One!"* 1554-3**

Now let us try to put this understanding in terms of today as used in a modern industrial nation. Let us begin with the phrase "Truth . . . is an earning." (262-19) Our earning is usually in the form of money. Perhaps we might consider truth as God's currency, and patience as truth-management, correlative of "money-management."

When thought of in these terms, one might begin to form questions, such as: What is the state of my truth-account? Is there a sufficient amount of truth on hand for my need? Is it in a form that can be readily used—or will it have to be converted from its present form into a more readily usable one? If it must be converted, how much delay will be involved before it can be used?

**. . . to know good and truth ye must live same. 1510-1**

**Know and behold the Lord is One. Thou art His son, a manifestation of His love, of His patience—in the earth. How art thou using same? 1537-1**

**. . . has it made in the experience of the individual a better neighbor, a kindlier friend, a more long-suffering one with those that would hinder? Doth it bring patience? Doth it bring love in any manifested form? 262-97**

**Only in the fruits of the spirit—as of long-suffering and patience and mercy and brotherly love and kindness and gentleness—may the true meaning of life's experience and the purposes of life, and in the associations with others, be understood. 1336-1**

**Ever, *ever*, the fruits of the Spirit in their awareness; long-suffering, brotherly love, patience, kindness, gentleness, *hope* and faith! If ye, in thy activities in any manner with thy fellowman, destroy these in the minds, in the hearts of thy fellowman, ye are not only slipping but ye have taken hold on the path of destruction. Then so live, so act, so *think* that others *seeing* thy good works, thy hopes that ye**

**bring, thy faith that ye manifest, thy patience that ye show, may *also* glorify Him. 826-11**

Are my truth accounts-receivable and accounts-payable in good order? Have there been investments (expressions of truth in thought, word, and deed) of a wise nature from which a good return might be expected? Or has there been a miserly handling of the truth currency so that there is stagnation? Has there been unwise handling which would cause a suffering of loss?

*But that [seed] on the good ground are they, which in an honest and good heart, having heard the word, keep it, and bring forth fruit in patience.* Luke 8:15 (KJV)

**Patience . . . becomes as the seed of faith, of hope, that blossom into those influences that make for harmony in the experience of others. 1193-1**

**Faint not because of disagreements or disappointments. Sow the seed of Truth, as ye are directed by the God-force within; then have the patience to leave the increase to the Giver of all good and perfect gifts.**

**Ye do not plant a seed and constantly scratch it up to see what has happened, but you do nourish it, you do water it, you do feed it in the way that is in keeping with the *nature* of that you are seeking to gain from same. 1151-12**

**For keeping the faith is just being one that shows in the experiences with the fellowman the things that become the fruits of the spirit; the fruits of the spirit of truth—gentleness, kindness, patience, long-suffering. For these bring their fruits into the hearts and the souls of men. Not that of satisfaction so much as contentment and peace, leaving with the Spirit of Truth the results that are to be accomplished. 1531-1**

So, whether our concepts are considered in symbols pastoral or symbols financial, in symbols ancient or symbols modern, the message remains the same:

**Through patience and endurance does the crown of joy, happiness, as the peace of His presence, give those blessings that are from His throne. His presence, with peace, is the promise of those who with patience endure the crosses that are set before thee day by day . . .**

**In patience does the knowledge of the peace and understanding of His presence come. An active force, not a passive one. Necessary that patience be exercised that ye know the hope, the faith, the knowledge, the understanding of His ways in the earth. 262-26**

For those of us trying to develop patience, there is one question which may be helpful, a question to be pasted on a mirror where it can be seen every morning and every evening at least:

**What would have been thy end had God grown impatient with thee? 5091-3**

# Service as an Ideal

## by Iverne C. Rinehart

HAVE YOU OFTEN found yourself asking: "What does it mean to serve—to be a servant? Am I serving? How can I serve?" All great religions and philosophies teach that man must serve his fellowman. We are also taught that a life of service is rewarding if the service is for its own sake and not for the glory of the server.

The cynic sneers at this philosophy saying it is only a ploy others use to get us to do their work for them—to "pull their chestnuts out of the fire." We cannot help but wonder, however, at the eventual fate of the cynic when he discovers he must account for the way in which he has spent his life. When he must finally admit that he put self first—that he believed in doing unto others before they could do unto him, the survival of the fittest, and other such selfish philosophies—will he then see how his opportunity was wasted and beg for a quick return to give it another try?

Most people who study the readings are concerned with their purposes, seeking true self-revelation. They have the desire to make this life a meaningful one and to *serve* with true unselfishness.

From the readings we find that questions of purpose were asked an individual who sought to devote herself to service by developing her psychic powers:

**Again this question should be answered within self: What is conscious service to the fellowmen? Impelling them to think as self thinks? Or is it to enable such to find their *own* expression with their conscious contact with psychic forces? 1376-1**

She was cautioned to be sure of her purpose and to eliminate all negative attributes from her life:

**Hence no hate, no dishonor; but patience, long-suffering, brotherly love, kindness, gentleness; not exalting of self but rather abasement of self that there may be the closer union, the closer walk with that I AM THAT I AM.**

**These be then those activities in which each soul may engage in a conscious material world. Not saying or acting unkind things. No harsh words. None of these are a part of the soul, that seeks for soul or psychic development. 1376-1**

She was then advised to accomplish her goal of psychic development by meditating, praying, and reading the Scriptures.

The question arises whether this same advice applies to others who, not seeking especially to increase their psychic abilities, are simply searching for ways by which they can be of more service.

It may be concluded from the readings that daily opportunities are provided at *any* level of development—that it is how we respond to each situation that determines our progress and our effectiveness as servants.

Inquirers were advised about careers in several specific fields:

*(Q) Where can I serve as a lawyer?*

**(A) *Begin* where you are, and the way is opened . . . 272-7**

**. . . the world's as big as ever! There [are] as many people hungry as ever. As many people need activities of those who are willing to spend themselves in giving for others that which will make for a better world in which to live. 419-3**

**For unless there is peace and happiness in the service . . . and unless such activities be prompted by higher or more constructive motives than material gains, little of peace and happiness may be the lot of the entity. 1447-4**

After an individual had been advised to serve through concert or stage work, this further advice was given:

*(Q) Any other advice for the body at this time?*

**(A) As given, look into self; know the purposes. By analyzing what has been the experience, see that the purposes are nigh unto the inner calls. Then, knowing ye are on the right track, or in the right direction, *apply* self. 1476-1**

The readings always directed inquiring individuals (and others by their examples) to look inward, to analyze their purposes and then to apply themselves in ways that would help the most people.

To a lady whose talents lay in writing, this advice was given:

**Then there must be through these very influences and channels an outlet, a manner in which these may find expression; which there is, in thy ability to *write beautiful* things that will act and react upon the minds and the hearts of others—those that may read,**

those that may make same to be a part of their experience by the very manner in which ye in loving care may show forth these in thy dealings with thy fellowman! . . . *open* thy heart, *open* thy abilities to others! 1567-2

When we falter and are tempted to give up too easily, it is helpful to look at the further advice as given to this woman:

Write—write—write! Though ye may tear up for a year, or for more than a year everything ye write giving expression to same, ye will find the abilities to bring into the experience and minds of others the joys that are not even comprehended in the present! 1567-2

The clear indication is that we are not to "weary in our well doing," but must be both persistent and consistent in our work for others—whatever our talents and abilities may be.

We often see businesses honor employees for their years of continuous service. Do we say a prayer of gratitude for those people and their devotion? Do we ever calculate the hours of faithful service those years represent? It can have a very humbling effect—especially if our own record is one of change, short-term occupations, and halfhearted service.

The readings point out that we must devote our *all* to being of service:

For until ye are willing to *lose* thyself in service, ye may not indeed know that peace which He has promised to give—to all. 1599-1

Some ways of serving seem so simple, so ordinary, that we may fail to recognize them as such. However, examples are cited in several readings:

. . . to do good, to be kind, to be gentle, to smile even when in pain, to look up when others are even tramping upon thine feet and give praise to Him in the inner self, is that He seeks for . . .

For as ye do it unto the least or the greatest, ye do it unto Him. For he that would be the greater among men is the servant of all! . . .

Be patient; be gentle; be kind. Show brotherly love. For what ye sow, ye reap. 815-3

For only as ye show mercy may it be shown to thee. Only as ye show patience, long-suffering, brotherly kindness, may these be shown to thee . . .

Be not then merely good, but be good for something—in *His* name! 1440-1

. . . as He has given, he that gives the cup of water shall not lose his reward . . . To the mother, as she cares for her offspring; though the trials of the material things may be heartrending, that smile, that kindly word gives hope to one who may even be burdened with the thought of how and in what manner the provisions of the day may be supplied! 1472-12

. . . thy prayer should ever be: "Lord, here am I— Use me in the way *Thou* seest that I may be the greater channel of blessings to those I meet day by day." 1599-1

From these readings we may infer that it is in our ordinary, *daily* associations with others that we constantly discover new avenues of service.

We are expected to examine our own inner selves through meditation and then take God as our partner, knowing that at any time we call on Him for help He will answer. Our daily prayer should be:

Use Thou me, O Lord, as Thou seest that I—as Thy servant—may serve the better! 1158-15

According to the readings, one of the vital ways to serve lies in helping others to understand themselves and their purposes.

*(Q) What important task, if any, have I yet to accomplish?*

**(A) As indicated; much work, much service is to be done in that of education to those that would know their relationships to Creative Forces. 1265-1**

To that individual who sought to develop her psychic abilities the reading made it clear how such development should be used and its relationship to A.R.E. work:

*(Q) In what way, if any, can [1376] be of help in the work of the Association for Research and Enlightenment, Inc.?*

**(A) By filling those purposes for individual application of the truths for individuals that may be presented from time to time, if the choice is set in truth. 1376-1**

As we seek ways to be of service to others we are cautioned to protect ourselves with a consciousness of the Christ Presence. Armed with His truth and with His protection, we should bring cheer, hope, help, faith, and courage to others. Every task accomplished strengthens us to take on an even more demanding one, and we gain strength by remembering that His Will is not a remote force, but very near—even within us—and that finding it is a simple exercise of faith.

# "There Is No Death"

by Renee C.M. Kessler

"Nothing is certain but death and taxes." This phrase is almost engraved into our consciousness. Can you enumerate how often you have heard it—or even possibly repeated it to others?

The whole statement is false!

Take taxes, for instance. According to our form of government, we can change the amount of taxes we pay, the frequency with which we pay taxes, and in certain instances either abolish them altogether or not pay them at all.

Death as we know it is not certain either. In a life reading Edgar Cayce was asked about overcoming death.

*(Q) Will I overcome death in this incarnation?*

**(A) There is no death . . . It is our promise, and**

**when ye abide in Him sufficient to that, ye with Him, as the resurrection, may indeed overcome death in a material sense. 5155-1**

In reading 2927-1, Edgar Cayce volunteered:

**Let that mind be in thee which was in Him, who gave: "I and the Father, God, are one." So become ye in thine own mind, as ye contribute, as ye attune thy inner self to those greater ideals; for it is not all of life just to live, nor yet all of death to die. For, they that put their whole trust in Him have passed from death unto life. And to such there is no death, only the entrance through God's other door.**

The facet of Life called Death is as simple as it is complex. It can be called "change." It can be called "departure." It can be called anything signifying transition or graduation from one level to another. It cannot be called "an End," however.

Why? There must be a reason for all these comings and goings. Edgar Cayce gave in reading 1947-3:

**Each entity enters materiality for a purpose. That all the experiences in the earth are as one is indicated by the desires, the longings as arise within the experience of that which makes for the growing, the knowing within self—the _mind!_ Thus does the entity, as a whole, become aware that it, itself, in body, mind and soul, is the result—each day—of the application of laws pertaining to creation, this evolution, this soul-awareness within, consciously manifested.**

**What is the purpose of entering consciousness? That each phase of body, mind and soul may be to the glory of that Creative Force in which it moves and has its being.**

After receiving one reading from Edgar Cayce, [2390] was told in a second reading about certain feelings and urges.

**Ye may ask—rightly—_why_ such urges are in the**

**experience so definitely as is being indicated. Because, as given, of a one cycle. For, remember—death in the material plane is birth in the spiritual-mental plane. Birth in the material plane is death in the spiritual-mental plane. Hence the reason that when those physical manifestations began to be impressed upon the brain centers—those portions of an individual entity that are a constant growth from first conception—there were impressions to hinder rather than aid the memory of other experiences. 2390-2**

This answer to certain influences in this life as well as the reasons for an inability to recall past lives of [2390] was very pointed. The reason was that the individual had to live this life now; work with the people contacted now; grow here and now. When the transition of this life was completed would be plenty of time to total and balance all the experiences felt through time.

Basically the reason for passing from the earth plane is that one has learned the lesson offered, or that one has not really gained from this experience. Not every individual leaves, however, because his work is completed. Reading 1408-2 was given posthumously at the request of a bereaved daughter:

**The body was so tired from the cares of the material world that physical reactions were in the heart; that [heart] had been so ready to open itself to the needs of each, not only of the family, but to all that knew, that even were acquainted with the body.**

**Yet it grew so weary with these cares that He, in His love, saw fit to let the separation come; that the soul might in peace *rest* in the arms of Him who is her Saviour—Jesus!**

**Hence you each should take the lesson of that courage, of that patience, of that forbearance, of that long-suffering, as a part of your own lives; and**

**let it become—as she manifested—the *experience* of the everyday life, in the dealings and in the associations with the fellow man.**

Surely this was a choice of the mother when she felt her children no longer needed her and knew the children themselves would never admit it. This is an example of the past age when social pressures were greater, when a woman, a mother, would be unable to leave her family by any means other than death. Had she done so—or even attempted to do so—social pressures as well as guilt feelings would have taken all the joy of her living as an individual.

Questions of "what happens after passing" have come from many petitioners. From reading 989-2:

**... a death in the flesh is a birth into the realm of another experience, to those who have lived in such a manner as not to be bound by earthly ties.**

The same question, reading 2147-1:

**For there is no death when the entity or the real self is considered; only the change in the consciousness of being able to make application in the sphere of activity in which the entity finds self.**

And in reading 900-17, the answer:

**The conscious mind forces either are in the soul's development, and in the superconsciousness, or left with that portion of material forces which goes to the reclaiming, or remoulding, of physical bodies, for indwelling of spiritual entities.**

That response indicates that depending upon the soul's needs, either the person takes on another body, or stays "in-between" gathering information for the next incarnation, if so desired.

The same person [900] requested more information two readings later.

*(Q) What form does the spirit entity take ... ?*

**(A) Taking that form that the entity creates for**

itself in the plane in which the existence is passed. As we have in the earth's plane the imagination, the mind of the individual pictures to itself, through its carnal relations, that condition to which its individual relation of entity assumes to itself, and the entity possessing that same ability to assume that position in which it may manifest itself according to its relative position to that merited condition in its existence. 900-19

So if a soul has passed through the earth plane, it takes a human form, improving that form if it so desires.

That same question, taken from the aspect of the organized church teachings was:

*(Q) Where are the dead until Christ comes? Do they go direct to Him when they die?*

(A) As visioned by the beloved, there are those of the saints making intercession always before the throne for those that are passing in and out of the inter-between; even as He, the Christ, is ever in the consciousness of those that are redeemed in Him.

The passing in, the passing out, is as but the summer, the fall, the spring; the birth into the interim, the birth into the material. 281-16

The reference to cycles is quite frequent. According to the readings all life is cycles of comings and goings.

Another question, based on the teachings of the organized church, was "Will we be punished by fire and brimstone?" The answer:

That as builded by self; as those emblematical influences are shown through the experiences of the beloved in that builded, that created. For, each soul is a portion of creation—and builds that in a portion of its experience that it, through its physical-mental or spiritual-mental, has builded for itself. And each entity's heaven or hell must, through *some* experience, be that which it has builded for itself.

Is thy hell one that is filled with fire or brimstone? But know, each and every soul is tried so as by fire, purified, purged; for He, though He were the Son, learned obedience through the things which He suffered. Ye also are known even as ye do, and have done. 281-16

In other words we make our own Heaven and/or Hell. Nor does this state wait until we have passed, or exist only on the other side. See *karma*, in the Edgar Cayce readings.

The readings always emphasized that the soul continues, that there is no end of existence.

*(Q) Explain the plane of spirit and soul forces, and what relation this plane has to earth. You will start with death, as we know it.*

(A) In that moment, as in birth, we have the beginning of an earthly sojourn, little or long, as time may be. So the birth into the spiritual plane begins with the death in earth plane; merely the separation of the spiritual and soul forces from the earthly connections. 900-19

Much help was given to people recently bereaved. Reading 1567-2 gave:

First we begin with the fact that God is; and that the heavens and the earth, and all nature, declare this. Just as there is the longing within every heart for the continuity of life.

What then is life? As it has been given, in Him we live and move and have our being.

Then He, God, *is!* Or Life in all of its phases, its expressions, is, a manifestation of that force or power we call God, or that is called God.

Then Life is continuous. For that force, that power which has brought the earth, the universe and all the influences in same into being, is a continuous thing— is a first premise.

All glory, all honor then, is *due* that creative force that may be manifested in our experiences as individuals through the manner in which we deal with our fellow man!

Then we say, when our loved ones, our heart's desires are taken from us, in what are we to believe?

This we find is only answered in that which has been given as His promise, that God hath not willed that any soul should perish but hath with every temptation, every trial, every disappointment made a way of escape or for correcting same. It is not a way of justification only, as by faith, but a way to know, to realize that in these disappointments, separations, there comes the assurance that He cares!

In reading 851-1, Edgar Cayce answered a mother who asked:

*(Q) Why was my son . . . taken so early in life?*

(A) Seek not to find that, that is best to be understood in Him!

Her next question was: "Did he leave a work unfinished that I could help to carry on? If not, who could carry it on?" The response:

Each have their individual portion in life. As each are in, or out, or pass through these activities, there are those that are brought in line to carry on in a way as is in keeping with those forces that direct, rule or govern, that as seen.

In other words, each of us has our own particular job, each of us has our own place. It is not for us to carry on others' work for emotional reasons only.

Reading 3954-1 answered the question about prayers for the passed:

Yea, pray oft for those who have passed on. This is part of thy consciousness. It is well. For, God is God of the living. Those who have passed through God's other door are oft listening, listening for the voice of those they have loved in the earth. The nearest and dearest thing they have been conscious of in earthly consciousness. And the prayers of others that are still in the earth may ascend to the throne of God, and the angel of each entity stands before the throne to make intercession. Not as a physical throne, no; but that consciousness in which we may be so attuned that we become one with the whole in lending power and strength to each entity for whom ye speak and pray.

For, where two or three are gathered together in His name, He is in the midst of them. What meaneth this? If one be absent from the body, He is present with His Lord. What Lord? If you have been the ideal, that one to whom another would pay homage, you are then something of the channel, of the ideal. Then thy prayers direct such an one closer to that throne of love and mercy, that pool of light, yea, that river of God.

Bereavement can be carried to such an extent that the soul remaining here stays in a half-living state:

*(Q) Is it well to foster the sense of continued communication with his [the deceased's] spirit while we are separated by "death" so-called?*

(A) If this is for a helpful experience to each, it is well. Let it rather be directed by that communion with Him who has promised to be *with* thee always! and hinder not then thy companion, but—in such associations and meetings—give the directions to the Holy One. 1782-1

Basically, this means to let go and let God. Don't tell God what to do!

Another reading, this for 1786-2, answered the question:

*(Q) Have I any further contact with my late husband . . . since he has passed on?*

(A) If that is the desire, it will continue to hang

on to same! If it is to be finished, and that which has been to be the development, then leave this aside.

The next question in 1786-2 was:

*(Q) Does he know of my prayers?*

(A) Do you wish him to? Do you wish to call him back to those disturbing forces, or do you wish the self to be poured out for him that he may be happy? Which is it you desire—to satisfy self that you are communicating, or that you are holding him in such a way as to retard? or hast thou *believed* the promise? Leave him in the hands of Him who is the resurrection! Then prepare thyself for same.

A reminder, a prodding, was given to those of us still on this side.

*(Q) How may I develop a spiritual consciousness, so as to make emotionally mine the belief that the so-called dead are alive; that my loved ones are near, loving me and ready to help me?*

(A) As has been given, know thy Ideal, in what thou hast believed; and then act in that manner, ministering to others. For perfect love casteth out fear, and fear can only be from the material things that soon must fade away. 1175-1

In reading 1947-3 Cayce reported:

And when this influence [of earthly experiences] ... becomes such, or so self-centered, as to lose sight of that desire, purpose, aim to be *to* the glory of its source, and seeks rather *for* self, then it errs in its application of the influences within its abilities for the application of mind within its own experience.

In reading 2927-1 the Cayce source volunteered:

Let that mind be in thee which was in Him, who gave, "I and the Father, God, are one." So become ye in thine own mind, as ye contribute, as ye attune thy inner self to those greater ideals; for it is not all of life just to live, nor yet all of death to die. For, they

**that put their whole trust in Him have passed from death unto life. And to such there is no death, only the entrance through God's other door.**

Time and again the readings obtained through Edgar Cayce insisted that the state we know as death is just a portion of another cycle. The cycle of earth is day-night-day-night. The cycle of our minds is waking-sleeping-waking-sleeping. The cycle of our purpose is work-rest-work-rest, or in our terminology, life-death-life-death. Our understanding to date has been based on the erroneous meaning of "death" as the "absence of life." The information we now have has changed that to mean "continuation of life."

# The Purpose of Meditation

### by Marlene Carpenter

IN ORDER TO see how meditation is a natural and fundamental part of man, it is first necessary to consider what man is. Man is a combination of body, mind, and soul—an interdependent being operating on all three levels, each closely tied to the other two. The body is our physical temple. The soul is our expression of Spirit in the earth plane. Mind is the important link between the two.

The Spirit, the Source of life, is one fundamental force—or creative energy—or God, manifesting in many forms. It can be likened to a tree: it has many branches, from which come many leaves, but the source of the life of the tree is one. All of our energy, whether it be work energy, sex energy, or anger energy, comes from only one source, for God *is* the energy Source in the universe.

We may look at the leaves of the tree separately, or at the branches separately; but when we step back to look at the entire tree, we see that it is indeed an integrated whole. The Edgar Cayce readings tell us that this oneness exists in the entire universe. Since we cannot step back and view the entire universe as we can a tree, this abstract concept should be taken as a logical inductive conclusion made by reason, or on faith. The readings insist that

**The first lesson for *six months* should be ONE— One—One—*One;* Oneness of God, oneness of man's relation, oneness of force, oneness of time, oneness of purpose, *oneness* in every effort—Oneness—Oneness! 900-429**

How does knowledge of the Oneness of God relate to meditation?

Knowledge alone is not enough; we need to *experience* the Oneness of God in order to *know*. Meditation helps us to get from the intellectual knowledge to the firsthand experience of that Oneness. Consider this example: before meeting a person for the first time, we may have some prior knowledge of him from what others have told us or what we have read about him. Once having *met* the person, however, we have *experienced* him to some degree, and each of us, in our own way, *knows* that person as we could not have before.

This is basically the difference between knowing about God and *knowing* God personally. This difference between knowing and experiencing is basically the difference between what the readings call the Christ Consciousness and the Christ Spirit. The Christ Consciousness is the soul's awareness of its oneness with God, imprinted on the mind and waiting to be awakened by the will. The Christ Spirit is the expression of this knowledge, through the fruits of the spirit: love, joy, peace, long-suffering, gentleness, goodness, faith (Gal. 5:22). Meditation helps us to get from the Christ Consciousness (the more intellectual level) to the Christ Spirit (the feeling/emotional level). The latter is really *knowing* in the true sense of the word.

The Christ Consciousness is that awareness waiting to be *awakened by the will.* The will is an attribute of the mind, and can direct its energies wherever the mind chooses. If we make the decision that we want to experience God, then the *will* directs our energies to that end. If we want things that are non-spiritual, then the will directs our energies to that end. We choose and then go in the direction that we have chosen. In meditation, which is directing the energies upward, we are creating that which we will become, that which we dwell on, and that which we have a strong desire to attain.

**For mind is the builder and that which we think upon may become crimes or miracles. For thoughts are things and as their currents run through the environs of an entity's experience these become barriers or stepping stones, dependent upon the manner in which these are laid as it were. 906-3**

"Directing our energies upward" means that meditation awakens within us that which is of greatest importance to us. It lifts and carries up our highest ideal, whether that be Christ-centered or earth-centered. Thus, it behooves us to think seriously about purifying our thoughts and emptying them of all negative and destructive purposes so that in meditation the positive and constructive will flow through us. Meditation is the access to the Throne of Grace, of Mercy, of Peace, of Understanding, within ourselves. But we will not arrive at that Throne if we carry within us a heavy burden of negative thinking. We must first empty ourselves of such thoughts, so the creative forces can work in and through us.

*Meditation is emptying* **self of all that hinders the creative forces from rising along the natural channels of the physical man to be disseminated through**

**those centers and sources that create the activities
of the physical, the mental, the spiritual man; properly done must make one *stronger* mentally, physically . . . 281-13**

Meditation, then, is directing the will toward an attunement to, an at-onement with, the God Force. We must want
to accept our divine heritage, which is to be co-creators
with God. We must want to use this universal and univer-
sally available energy for the purpose of lifting up ourselves and everyone we encounter. We must want, deep in
our inmost heart, to express God in this earth—to bring
the Infinite into finite expression.

Meditation is not withdrawal. It is contacting the God
within and becoming a channel for the God Force in a very
real and substantial way.

**That He gave of old is as new today as it was in the
beginning of man's relationship or seeking to know
the will of God, if ye will but call on Him *within* thine
inner *self!* Know that thy body is the temple of the
living God. There He has promised to meet thee!
281-41**

Through the practice of meditation we begin to express
in small, subtle ways the fruits of the Spirit. We shouldn't
expect tremendous changes, but a gradual unfoldment of
that beautiful, unique being within us.

**Not that some great exploit, some great manner
of change should come within thine body, thine mind,
but line upon line, precept upon precept, here a
little, there a little. For it is, as He has given, not the
knowledge alone but the practical application—in
thine daily experience with thy fellow man—that
counts. 922-1**

There are those who believe that meditation is an end
in itself; that the purpose of meditating is to find a few
minutes each day to be at peace. This is well, but mislead-
ing. Peace and serenity are side effects of meditation, but

not the goal. Meditation is a means or method for a far more noble and rewarding experience than a half hour of peace and quiet. The practice of meditation must gradually, subtly, and cumulatively lead to a new and better way of life. This is the *only criterion* of successful meditation: a changed life in accordance with the fulfillment of the highest ideal we have set for ourselves. The fruits of meditation occur not during those few minutes we set aside for the practice of meditation, but during the rest of the day. Living meditation is efficiency, love, and devotion to *whatever* we are doing at any time, whether it be washing dishes, mowing the lawn, or solving a problem on the job.

As these results come into our lives, we also notice that the practice of meditation ceases to become discipline. It becomes rather a yearning, a desire to be with a Loved One (the Lord) for a few minutes each day because it is such a natural part of man and his life in this plane. Manifesting the Spirit in the three-dimensional world is man's purpose in the earth plane. When that purpose is seen to be bearing fruit, what greater joy and yearning could we have than to return to meditation, from which it all springs.

Meditation is a *natural* practice. The definition quoted earlier states that

**Meditation is emptying self of all that hinders the creative forces from rising along the natural channels of the physical man . . .**

This desire of the soul is just as natural as the physical desires of the body such as hunger, thirst, and sex.

**Don't seek for unnatural or supernatural! It is the natural—it is nature—it is God's activity! His associations with man—His *desire* to make for man a way for an understanding! 5754-3**

As we begin to feel the truth of this statement through the practice of meditation, we begin to realize that it is the way to rid ourselves of turmoil, strife, and disappointment. The thought patterns that have chained us to these negative and fruitless obstacles are dissolved, and we are re-stored to an awareness of our true nature.

**And whatever may be the choices of others, let self determine: "Others may do as they may, but as for me—I will serve a living God. I will manifest love, I will manifest patience, I will manifest long-suffering, I will manifest brotherly love."**

**And in so doing there will come in the daily experience that which will bring from turmoils, strifes, heartaches, disappointments, those promises as He hath given, "My peace I leave with you"—not as the world knoweth peace, but that as satisfies the longings of the soul and makes for that experience in the lives of individuals when the outlook becomes more hopeful in Him, in Life, in thy Brother, in thy associations. 1326-1**

There is a difference between prayer and meditation. Prayer is active: talking to God, turning our consciousness to Him, asking Him for advice or help, seeking Him out. Meditation, on the other hand, is a passive listening—a receptive attitude, in which we wait for His answer. It is becoming quiet so that we may attune ourselves to Him and hear His answer. We often do implore and invoke God's assistance, but then keep our minds so actively dwelling on the problem (which we have supposedly turned over to Him), that we don't give Him a chance to answer us. But God *will* answer, if we would only listen. The answer may not always come in the meditation, but meditation will open the way so that the answer can be heard. It may come in a dream, in a new idea, or as a "voice out of the blue." Prayer and meditation go hand in hand.

There are three stages to the prayer-meditation process. First comes the stilling of the body and the speaking of the opening prayer. This can be a prayer of protection, or a prayer of thanksgiving; it can be a prayer in which we ask that God take over some important concern of ours, or it can be a general prayer of invitation. The Lord's Prayer is excellent for any and all of these concerns. Whatever prayer we use, we must be certain that we are *sincere* in wanting to contact the Father and learn from Him. Any prayer we utter should be spoken (or thought) slowly and with feeling.

The second stage in the process is often called "entering the silence." When we enter the silence, we keep in mind, as on a screen in front of the mind, an affirmation or thought of high ideal. We slowly let that affirmation fade into the background as we go deeper and deeper into the silence, which is the contact with the God within. Thoughts seem to crop up which have no bearing on the spiritual goal: the shopping list for tomorrow, the letter to write, the words of a friend. We can gently bring the mind back to focus on the affirmation. The affirmation is that which we are building in our consciousness and that to which we return when we find ourselves slipping out of the silence. If one is unaccustomed to entering the silence, mind and body might rebel for a while because it's a new habit pattern that has not yet been assimilated by the three-dimensional being (body, mind, and soul). Patience, persistence, and perseverance are necessary.

During this stage of entering the silence, energy will begin to build up. This is Creative Energy, the God Force within meeting the God Force without. This energy working in and through the body must be dispersed, and so we enter the third stage of the process, called the intercessory or healing prayer.

At this time we ask that God send this energy to those in some need, or simply to those we love; we can even let God decide where to send it if we don't want to send it anywhere in particular.

We *never* send a healing prayer to another for a specific healing to be done; i.e., that his liver condition gets better, or that he become more religious, or the like. We want

God's will to be done and perhaps the liver condition is only a symptom of a far greater illness of which we are unaware. We are meddling when we pray for specifics in this way, especially where healing is concerned; no one is a good enough physician or psychiatrist—even those M.D.s who are expert in their field—to know precisely what the individual needs in the way of healing. Only God knows that. This type of meddling (although often done with the best intentions) can be extremely dangerous. The safest, most productive prayer that we can offer, at the end of the prayer-meditation process, in order to share the energy raised within you, is to pray that the Christ Light and the Christ Love surround and enfold certain people or situations or organizations. Then we speak their names, audibly or silently. In this way, when that person is ready for God's healing stream of energy to flow through him, there will be more than ample supply waiting for him to use.

This process may take only fifteen minutes a day but should be as close to the same time each day as possible. One can build up his time as he feels the desire to do so. The rate of increase, and even the desire to increase, depends on the individual. It is far better to meditate consistently once a day at the same time for fifteen minutes than to be sporadic and haphazard in the effort. The fruits of contact with the God Force do not depend on how *long* we are with Him, but that we get to *Him* regularly.

Meditation is a practice for the purpose of attuning ourselves to the God within. Because God is One, we learn to experience this unity within our own bodies, our lives, and our affairs. We even learn to experience our oneness with other people and begin to see, for example, that we are in the other, and the other is in us, because we all have one fundamental, spiritual Source—God.

# Perfect Understanding:
# What Is Truth?

## by Charles Sinex

EDGAR CAYCE, LECTURING in a conscious state about truth, once said, "Life in its projection into the material plane has been a constant growth. Then if we are to believe the things that have been presented to us—and *as they are presented to us*—we know that even Truth itself may be a *growth* into that understanding which we will be able to apply in our everyday life."

Most Christians accept the words of Jesus as truth; but the understanding of Jesus' sayings varies with the individual. It is not unusual for one religious institution to disagree with another over the "correct" interpretation of a truth spoken by Jesus. This leaves the individual who is seeking confused as to which is right, or whether there is only one which is right.

The individual who is seeking not only truth but the correct understanding of the truth is confronted by a myriad of books and often disagreeing authorities. The readings have proved to be helpful to many seeking the truth or the right understanding of truth. The following excerpt illustrates that truth grows as our understanding of it grows:

**That that is Truth is growth! For what is truth today may be tomorrow only partially so, to a developing soul!**

**So, the ideal is that which—as truth—grows towards a constructive nature in the experience of each soul; not self-indulgence, not self-glorification, not self-gratification, but that which *being* the basis for expression may be glorified, may be kept as a standard—*not* self! 1297-1**

In P.D. Ouspensky's book, *The Psychology of Man's Possible Evolution*, the terms "knowledge," "understanding," and "being" are discussed: " . . . there are two sides of man which must develop in the normal course of his evolution: knowledge and being. But neither knowledge nor being can stay still or remain in the same state. If either of them does not grow bigger and stronger, it becomes smaller and weaker.

"Understanding may be compared to an *arithmetical mean* between knowledge and being. It shows the necessity for a simultaneous growth of knowledge and being. The growth of only one and diminishing of another will not change the arithmetical mean."

Most people will agree that understanding is certainly dependent upon knowledge, but few take into consideration the quality of a person's *being*, which could explain why so many people perceive the same knowledge in so many different ways. Their prejudices, attitudes, and character cause each of them to view the same knowledge from different perspectives.

This viewpoint could give a deeper insight to the following selection:

**This in itself should convince anyone of the sense-lessness of denominationism, and how hard for the entity to give it up! Yet the growth has gradually come. For God is not a respecter of persons, it is true. Neither does He care in the way that individuals do for a name, or as to what people will say. Truth is truth and it convicteth the soul. The soul alone is eternal. All that is of earth-earthy is carnal and passeth away. 3179-1**

It has been said that knowledge becomes understanding through experience. This could mean applying newly received knowledge to past or present experiences to see them in a new perspective. In school, students are given knowledge on chemistry and physics; in the laboratory, their experiments show how the knowledge works.

Teachers realize that the *experience* of the knowledge is fundamental to the *understanding* of it.

While many systems could be devised for classifying levels of understanding, we examine here only literal, psychological, and spiritual categories. There are, however, many degrees within each of these categories. As a frame of reference let us consider a literal understanding to represent an external manifestation of truth, one that can be demonstrated in the physical world. We will use "psychological understanding" to represent a truth which can be experienced internally. A spiritual understanding will be defined as a truth revealed to one's inner self as a sudden insight not coming from one's ordinary self but from a higher source.

The following extracts give additional insight into the three worlds of matter, mind, and spirit:

**For matter is the expression of spirit *moving* in the material world. The mind is the builder in which there are all of its phases and manifestations. And thou hast set before thee a *great* undertaking. Be thou faithful to that which has been entrusted unto thee.**

**From whom? From the Creative Forces that find manifestation in thine inner self. 520-4**

*(Q) By what steps are developed the powers of spiritual healing?*

**(A) Through spiritual growth. By what powers doth a grain of corn maintain its ability to produce corn; that divine gift to the first corn? By not trying to be something else than a grain of corn! Thus may there come an understanding to any soul, to any that will say "Use me, O God, as Thou will." But not remaining idle! 705-2**

**That which is expressed or manifested in spirit, without taking body or form, is of the spirit; yet may be manifested in the experience of an individual. 262-78**

New knowledge can lead to new understandings with a resulting change in being. Our present level of being, as it is manifested, is in the earth plane. Knowledge received and understood, when applied to soul development, can transform our level of being to a higher state.

This process can be illustrated on a small scale in our own lives as we understand and apply the teaching of Jesus Christ who said: "A new commandment I give unto you, that ye also love one another." (John 13:34) By placing the welfare of others ahead of our own, we change our way of life by becoming better persons and blessings to all we contact.

Knowledge gained which is applied to aggrandizement of self's own desires will lead to a continuation of present level of being or a decline in level of being. Knowledge received which is misunderstood or misapplied is of no advantage to self and might result in great harm to others and our future state of being. The Edgar Cayce readings counseled on right use of new knowledge and understanding:

**Then, use thyself just as the source of thy knowl-**

edge. For in the perfect understanding of the emotions, of the causes, of the hopes and desires of self (not in a selfish manner, but as a constructive force—as has been thy experience through the sojourns in the earth), the entity may come to be the greater influence for hope, for good in the experience. 1998-1

Study, then, *patience*, long-suffering, gentleness, kindness. For these are the fruits of the Spirit and bring in their application experiences worthy of consideration in the minds and hearts of those who would know the right way. 470-14

For as the elements of the material world represent an association with the individual life, know these need, these will have, these *must* have, their understanding; *else* we may find those things that become as ashes of despair . . . as the foulness of misunderstanding! 601-11

To summarize, one may compare truth to a perfectly cut diamond. As one gazes upon a single facet of this gem, he beholds a beautiful sight and derives much meaning from what he beholds. But as one turns the diamond and gazes upon another facet, he sees another meaning, which appears to be a different truth, although it is the same stone. This process continues until he finally sees many meanings to this perfect truth. Perfect understanding comes when one can see all of these meanings simultaneously.

# Abiding Concern:
# An Ideal for Business

◆

## by Jerry D. Oakes

As ONE LEAVES the restored area of Old Sturbridge Village, Massachusetts, there is a sign for all to read, which bears the following inscription: "The New England of the period you are leaving made many contributions to the America we know. Town meeting democracy, universal common school education and an *abiding concern for the welfare of one's fellow men* became underlying principles of the American way of life as New Englanders migrated to other parts of the land." (Italics mine) The idea that our founding fathers had an abiding concern for others' welfare as a principle of life caught my attention, touching something deep within me.

Relationships have changed from those days of direct contacts with neighbors, to organizations, corporations, and institutions interacting with invoices, packing slips, checks, purchase orders, and a myriad of other cleverly devised systems to meet the demands of the business structures we have created. Because of this relative lack of personal contact in the dealings of modern businesses, responsibility for ethical behavior is oftentimes obscured. There is genuine confusion about *who* is responsible.

The Edgar Cayce material speaks directly to all aspects of our activity, and corporate life is certainly included. The readings can greatly aid in reestablishing the necessity of "abiding concern" for our fellow man.

Organizations cannot be allowed to become, in our consciousness, automatons or lifeless forces where service to individuals is impossible. The corporation is, in legal terms, a creature of the law. To consider it without human traits or without motivations behind its workings is to make the same mistake the Trojans made with Ulysses. The seemingly inanimate horse was rolled inside the walls of Troy with most unexpected results. That which seemed to be a lifeless creation of man proved otherwise. Although businesses are inanimate structures, they contain vital and creative forces.

**Be sure, then, that the business, as well as self, takes care and is mindful of the soul—for the spirit that maketh alive manifests through that of the *individual* soul, and a business—a large business, even—may or may not have a soul. A *soul* meaning that which, in this sense, lives *on* in the lives, in the minds and hearts, of those served by that business. Be mindful of that! 5417-2**

It is quite clear that the high spiritual message in the Cayce readings is service to others—selfless service. Those of us in business are often confounded by our choices and the how of weaving service into the fabric of our corporate beings. The ideal for business motivation could be expressed:

[Give] due consideration to the consumer, to the producer, to every branch; not top-heavy anywhere, not lacking in service anywhere; but as each would have the other do to them, do they even so to every association. 257-181

And specifically this advice was given to an individual:

Not that the having of a factory is necessarily evil, a factory that may be an outlet for the activities; but the use of same, the application of same in the relationships to the activities of the body—as have been so oft indicated—may be evil. For unless each executive in charge of affairs in the whole organization is imbued with the spirit (not merely the idea but the spirit) of cooperation, or the ideal of those that are the leading factors . . . there will be many, many a headache!

In considering then, think on these things seriously. Each head of each department—not merely the financiers (these, to be sure) but the finishings, the executives, the sales—all branches. And if this is done, it may be well with all. 257-181

The accountant, in working with figures, may find it difficult to feel a human relationship in them, but figures are representatives of physical things, and they explain and describe relationships in the same way as the spoken or written word. The balance sheet and profit and loss statement express how effectively people have utilized their resources of people, material, equipment, and money in a certain time period. And by the same rationale, behind the equipment, material, and money are more people with whom relationships are necessary. Ultimately, man is behind every business system and activity. The workings of mindforce are in everything:

. . . life in its activity is the expression of the divine influences in a material world. And individuals . . . may, through the drawing wholly, solely, upon the

**Creative Forces within, *change* their own surroundings, their *own* vibrations, within their bodies! 404-3**
Bodies, in this reading, could be individual or collective, as expressed by business structures.

We should consider the position we occupy as an opportunity for service.

**In service to mankind, is first gaining the understanding, the knowledge of self, the needs—and little by little; not *big* things—for these are the outgrowth of the small things; for acorns are not timbers, neither is the electron the large dynamo; neither is the stone the center of the building—yet these added to, grown in grace, in knowledge, in understanding, become the basis for *all* things. 520-2**

## What Is Success?

"*Undershaft:* Is there anything you know or care for?

"*Stephen:* I know the difference between right and wrong.

"*Undershaft:* You don't say so! What, no capacity for business, no knowledge of law, no sympathy for art, no pretension to philosophy, baffled all the lawyers, muddled all the men of business, and ruined most of the artistic; the secret of right and wrong. Why, man, you are a genius, a master of masters, a god!" (*Major Barbara* by G. B. Shaw)

Shaw's cynicism, or, perhaps, teaching, through his character Undershaft, expresses a notion that applied ethics in business, law, philosophy, and art will be the undoing of the practitioner. Yet he allows that the possessor of the understanding of right and wrong stands above all men. The one who applies right in all activity to the maximum of consciousness is certainly a master of himself in accordance with principle.

**For the earthly or material gains must be the outcome, the result of a spiritual, a mental purpose, a**

**desire, an exemplification of same in the dealings and relationships with others, for it to be a permanent or growing experience, and to not become more and more of such a fluctuating nature as to continue to bring greater and greater confusion—until, in the aims and purposes, there is lost the real desire for which the soul sought material manifestations. 1849-2**

Perhaps some men and women in business have been "muddled" because cheating, half-truths, deception, and unethical behavior have become commonplace. Honesty has in some cases become a matter of convenience rather than an absolute principle to which adherence is demanded by an individual of himself.

Is it possible to make absolute honesty a business virtue? Can such a creed be used as a business tool without an adverse effect on business goals and profits? The Edgar Cayce readings suggest we should examine our business, as well as all of our activity, this way.

**Look into the hearts of those that apparently are successful in material things, and unless such successes are founded in the spirit of justice, mercy, love and long-suffering and brotherly kindness, they must fade and fall away. Yet, if they are builded in these things that are the fruits of the spirit, they will grow and blossom as the Rose of Sharon; and ever will thyself in the spirit of thy angel that stands before His face find *pleasure* and grace and mercy in the eyes and heart of thine Maker. 531-3**

Jesus Christ makes it clear that our needs will be met with abundance and beauty by being faithful to the true principles of life (Matthew 6:25-34). These principles are absolute and not relative to a situation. When a choice is to be made in dealing with a customer, a fellow worker, or an employee, the principles involved are not changed or altered by the expressions, "But this is different; this is business," or "Business is business." These fallacious thoughts are designed to excuse or lead the user of them away from principle.

**And if an individual is attempting to comply with the spiritual, the mental and the material laws as one, and thus fulfill the purposes for which it as an individual is given an opportunity in a material plane, it *will* consider from the *spiritual* angle—and thus *not* the greater stress upon the material. 670-10**

The readings show that an individual can be in harmony in most any place or position in business in which he finds himself.

**The analysis has been given as to the activities in business. The present associations and activities we find are well, and will lead to those things that will bring for the present experience the material needs of the mental successes in thine associations with thy fellow man. 531-3**

## Profits and People

Many countries today have allowed a shift from the "abiding concern" principle to a "profits precede people" philosophy. This has not been a deliberate process, but perhaps the insidious forces of self-gratification through corporate structures have brought it about. Man cannot serve God and mammon, and if the Christ of God is in every man we should ever be alert to any act which in our consciousness would be *for* profits and *anti* people. An example of this would have to be the practice of layoffs where profits are threatened. The answer is not an easy one because a decision may require cutting of dividends on which people are dependent versus laying off those who are dependent on the job. But only the management individuals involved can answer within themselves what is right for them in each case. The arguments pro or con in the hiring and firing of people as well as other business decisions would go on endlessly. But Hugh D'Andrade reports in his book, *Charles Fillmore* (founder of Unity), a story which illustrates a point we might all consider. D'Andrade tells how an appeal for a job would always touch Fillmore in a tender spot. He would create a job, or ask his wife Myrtle to do so, or appeal to a co-worker, "Give her a job." The answer to him was that there were no jobs to give. "Create a job for her," said Charles. "She needs money in order to get her dental plates. She is toothless. Give her a job." Can there really be an error in this action if William Law is correct when he writes, "All errors are the want of love"?

Fortunately, there are many business movements in the United States where people appear to be concerned with spreading kindness and love. One major corporation has built several new plants in the last three years where there are no time cards, no rules on length of rest or lunch breaks, and several other policies promoting trust and honesty. These are judged to be practical, because the plants are profit-producing as well as dignity-promoting for the people. There is a president of a major U.S. company who spends much time speaking with employees and other groups about business ethics and their application in their working lives. There is much hope and reason to be optimistic about the possibility of the Christ Spirit becoming manifest in our "creature of the law" as well as within the people who operate and make the "creature" alive and vital.

## Business Advice

Mr. Cayce gave several readings with specific advice for individuals in business:

**. . . choose as self would see. Not that as will bring**

for just the money, but that that will bring into the lives of individuals that which may help physically, mentally, the soul, the development of many. 520-2

And to one hoping to build a practice he answered—

*(Q) How am I able to establish a clientele for these offices?*

(A) . . . Let each client, each person ye serve, be that as He gave—"He that would be the greatest among you will be and is the servant of all." 2275-1

To another—

*(Q) Please advise me as to my business.*

(A) . . . in thy conversation, remember—let each customer, not only in the material way but in the mental, feel refreshed from being in thy presence; for thy conversation is to be helpful—not merely "small talk." 2438-1

To one who had aspirations—

*(Q) Have I the proper mental and physical quali-fications to succeed as an executive?*

(A) You have the mental and physical qualifica-tions to succeed, if ye will but look within. Who is the greater executive than thy God? Who may guide thee aright greater than He? What thou lackest He may add to thee, if ye seek in that manner. For His promise has been, "If ye will be my children, I will be thy God, and I will raise thee up that none shall say ought against thee, and those that would hurt or make thee afraid shall become as naught." Stand . . . with the *truth*, putting on the armor of God; and thou shalt be strong in thy might! 802-2

There are many more readings, all tailored to individual circumstances and needs, for those in business. They ad-vise that the persons look within, hold to the high ideal of the Christ in their lives, and know not separation of self from others, but Oneness. There is no substitute for abso-lute honesty in all dealings in business and to compromise or to act with the belief that "business is business" is a deception which is counter to a spiritual path.

Here is an advanced question from one in business who was seeking the spiritual path:

*(Q) How can I best serve God and live a full and free life with perfect self-expression and adequate supply to enable me to function without worry and anxiety?*

The answer is not only good business advice but applies to all activity.

**(A) As it becomes or behooves one in one's preparation for any specific mental or material activity, first make the preparations from within. And whom thou would serve at least be on the same *speaking* associations with, that is necessary for *every* activity in that direction. This, as in material surroundings, insures or fortifies one as to one's success. There has been and is ever the promise to every soul that He, thy Father, thy God, will meet thee in thy holy temple. Then accept same. Prepare self. Dedicate self; making those necessary activities for insuring self of that influence, that activity on the part of self, and there needs be little fear—*ever*—to enter. For he that does so doubting already invites that which would bring corruption, dissension. But he that does so in the assurance that the promises are true, the promises are thine *own*, is insuring self and making secure. 877-2**

# The Lord Will Provide

## by Marcia Popa

"THEREFORE DO NOT be anxious, saying, 'What shall we eat?' or, 'What are we to put on?' (for after all these things the Gentiles seek); for your Father knows that you need all these things. But seek first the kingdom of God and his justice, and all these things shall be given you besides." (Matt. 6:31)

In these days of skyrocketing prices perhaps you, *Journal* reader, can profit from my experiences. If you have not, as yet, tried economic healing, why not give it a try? You may be pleasantly surprised at the results. I was.

One spring afternoon a few years ago, Marty, a neighbor of mine, mentioned she had to set out her tomato plants. Set out tomato plants? I asked. What a waste of time. All you have to do is go to the store, select the tenderest, juiciest, reddest tomatoes you can find, plunk down some change, and you're on your way to gastronomic delight.

In early August of that same year, during my weekly sojourn at the supermarket, the prices on summer tomatoes were far higher than they had been the previous year—so were lettuce, radishes, cabbage, green beans, and all the other vegetables my family and I enjoy eating. A thought floated through my mind—maybe Marty's idea about the tomato plants wasn't so bad. After all, we do own the vacant lot next to our house. Maybe I could spade up some of it and put in a few tomato plants—maybe some lettuce and green beans.

I mentioned this to Marty on one of my jaunts to her house for a cup of coffee, all the while thinking to myself, "Food is expensive, but summertime is a time to be enjoyed—not a time to be digging in the dirt, weeding, and working your fool head off."

I didn't plant a garden—not that year.

On a sunny morning in May of the following year, I was again coffee-klatsching with Marty. As I set my cup on her kitchen table, I said, "Really, Marty, one of these days I am going to put in a garden. The price of food is getting too high. Forty-nine cents for a head of lettuce! Can you imagine?"

Marty looked up, wiping bismark crumbs from her mouth. "Tomorrow is the first of June. If you're going to plant that vegetable garden you're always talking about, you'll have to get started now. I have some seeds left over from my garden. Come on, let's go!" Marty gathered the brightly colored packets of seeds from her cupboard shelf. "Where do you want to start digging?"

"Let me finish my coffee," I protested, a little shocked that she would take my casual remark so seriously.

Marty, standing at the open door with seed packets in hand, said, "Come on, you'll have to hurry. You have a lot of work to do today." Marty marched briskly toward my house as I meekly followed.

When we arrived at my front walk, she asked, "Where is your spade?"

"Spade?"

"Yes, spade. You do have one, don't you?"

"It's in the garage."

I went to the garage, brought the spade to Marty, and pointed out the spot I thought most suitable for a vegetable garden. She dug the spade into the freshly mowed grass. Soon mounds of rich, black earth appeared where an hour earlier was a neatly manicured lawn.

"I have to go now. Ronnie and Debbie will be coming home for lunch," she said, handing the spade to me.

What have I got myself into? I thought. I can't put the lawn back together again. I'll have to go through with this "garden thing." There's no other way.

I dug the shovel into the sod and by nightfall the earth was ready to receive the seeds Marty had given me. The ground was ready; I was exhausted. I had worked most of the day, dug up a large part of the empty lot, and my body ached. I promised myself I would never again say I was going to do something unless I really *wanted* to and *intended* to do it. That night I dreamed I was being chased by gigantic tomatoes, green peppers, and stalks of celery.

The next morning I looked out the kitchen window. It wasn't all a dream. The lawn had been replaced by what was the beginning of a mini-farm. It was ready and waiting for me! I marked off the rows and planted the seeds.

After the seeds were snugly in the soil, it occurred to me something was missing. I thought of my conversation with Marty the previous year when she mentioned she had to set out her tomato plants.

So I paid a visit to the neighborhood lawn and garden center and hurried home to set out my tomato plants.

By the middle of June, green sprouts were poking their heads out of the ground. I was proud of every one of them.

Much to my surprise, I discovered I enjoyed working in the soil.

As the summer progressed, what once was covered with that green stuff that had to be continually mowed started rapidly maturing into plants: tomatoes, cucumbers, green beans, zucchini, and almost every other vegetable imaginable.

In mid-August I started reaping the rewards of my efforts. Each meal on our family table was graced with luscious vegetables fresh from the garden. I shared the over-supply with relatives and friends and noticed my grocery bills were lower than they had been for some time.

In my A.R.E. Study Group we had occasionally discussed economic healing and I had been applying some of the principles with varying degrees of success. Could this be part of it? I wondered. Well, why not? I could not have grown all this food without His help, could I? And, working hand in hand with nature, I could not help but feel closer to God. This, I concluded, truly is economic healing, although perhaps not in exactly the way I had anticipated.

Toward the end of August, during a dinner that included fresh, crunchy salad, tender young green beans, and zucchini dripping with cheesy sauce, my husband, Gene, remarked, "I thought you would give up this garden idea after a few weeks, but I'll have to admit I was wrong. You've done a good job."

I smiled my appreciation. "To tell the truth, when I first started the garden, I wasn't sure I'd be able to stick it out."

As Gene reached for another helping of zucchini he asked, "But what are you going to do to keep all those vegetables from going to waste? We can only eat so much. We don't have a freezer and this is not the time to start learning how to can. You've never done any canning, and besides, there is a shortage of jars. You can't buy them in any of the stores."

"Never mind," I said. "God gave us the vegetables. He won't let them go to waste."

Gene looked at me as though I had lost my senses. "Are you talking about that 'Lord will provide' stuff again?"

"That's right," I replied, trying to sound confident.

"Well, I believe in God, but I think you're carrying all that a little too far."

I had put my foot in it. I had met with some degree of success with economic healing, but a freezer? I didn't know. I just didn't know. I had a little money put aside. Maybe I could buy a freezer!

The next day I started looking at prices in the stores. The freezers were far more expensive than I had expected. I drove home wondering what to do next.

When I arrived home, I went straight to the garden. I looked at the bright red tomatoes, the enormous zucchini plants, the twining vines with cucumbers hiding under the dark green leaves. Then I looked up into the bright sky and said out loud, "Okay, God, now it's up to You."

As I turned to enter the house, I noticed an enormous head of cabbage ripe for plucking. The thought occurred to me that I could use the cabbage for sarma (a European dish, a favorite of my husband's) for next Sunday's dinner. I had ground meat in the small freezing compartment of my refrigerator, but I didn't have a picnic ham. If I could grow picnic hams in the garden . . . Thoughts were flitting through my mind when I suddenly heard a voice calling, "Marcia, Marcia."

Marty appeared from nowhere. "Marcia, are you all right?" she questioned. "I've been watching you from across the street for the past ten minutes. First you were talking to the sky and now you're staring at a head of cabbage."

"Oh, I'm fine," I replied, trying to conceal my embarrassment. I hoped Marty was the only one who had noticed me. I thought it best not to mention my idea of growing picnic hams in the garden!

"Marcia, I think you've been working too hard," she said, looking at me curiously. "I'm taking my kids to the neighborhood carnival tonight. Why don't you and your son join us?"

"That sounds like fun, Marty," I replied. "We'll join you."

That evening Marty and I, with the youngsters, went off to the festivities. When we arrived, the carnival was bustling. We rode the whip, the Ferris wheel, and the rocket. We watched while the children played ring toss—the object of the game being to toss a ring on a cane. If the ring landed on a cane, it became the player's prize.

Marty wandered to the adjacent booth while the children tossed rings. "It's only a dime, Marcia. Why don't you take a chance?" she called.

"All right," I said as I walked over to the booth. "I haven't tried my luck at any games tonight. I may as well take at least one chance before I leave."

The booth attendant was getting ready to spin the wheel as I approached. I noticed dimes placed on almost all the numbers except for one vacant spot, number 17. As I put a dime on number 17 the attendant began spinning the wheel. "Round and round she goes, where she stops . . . " he rambled on. Click—click—click went the wheel. "Number *17!* Number 17 wins—a picnic ham!"

Marty and I gathered the children together (along with their newly acquired canes) and we started home. We said good-bye to Marty and her youngsters at their front walk.

When we arrived home I said to Gene, "Well, the Lord provided again."

"What are you talking about?" he asked.

"Well, He's given us a lovely garden. And I needed a picnic ham for Sunday dinner and He saw to it that I won it!"

"*You* grew the vegetables. And as far as the ham is concerned, that was luck," Gene replied obstinately.

August slid into September and the Saturday after Labor Day, Gene said, "Let's take a ride and see my brother, Pete, and his new wife, Linda." We had not seen them since their wedding.

As I walked out to the car, leaves crunched under my feet. Driving along the highway, I noticed the leaves were turning from green to the beautiful brown, yellow, and red shades of autumn.

When we arrived, Pete's son, Mike, greeted us at the door. Linda served us coffee and orange chiffon cake.

After a few minutes of friendly conversation, Pete asked, "Gene, do you know anyone who needs a freezer? We have two and want to get rid of one."

Almost choking on the cake, trying to get the words out, Gene and I cried in unison, *"We do!"*

Pete and Linda each owned a freezer prior to their marriage. Two such appliances were one too many.

"How much do you want for it, Pete?" Gene eagerly asked.

"I didn't say I want to sell it. We don't need it. If you can make use of it, you're more than welcome to it. It's in the garage. Come on, I'll show it to you."

Pete led us into the garage where he had stored the extra freezer. It was exactly like one I had admired a few weeks earlier in one of the stores, and couldn't afford.

A few days later, Pete and Gene moved the freezer from Pete's garage to our house. As my harvest came in, I prepared the vegetables and froze them. The freezer was large, and after the tomatoes, parsley, green beans, winter squash, summer squash, and peppers had been frozen, there was some space still available. That was quickly remedied.

One day Gene came home carrying an enormous box. He sat it on the kitchen table and said, "Well, here's something to fill up the freezer."

"What do you mean?"

"Open the box."

The box contained an assortment of foodstuffs: hot dog

and hamburger buns, a variety of pastries, a dozen or so frozen pizza pies, a few packages of hot dogs, and two boxes of ice cream bars.

"Where did they come from?" I asked.

"It was intended for a company benefit, but the company over-ordered. They asked a guy I know to dispose of it in any way he saw fit. He asked me if I knew of anyone that wanted it and I told him I sure did. Me!"

I filled the remaining space in the freezer and shared the excess with Marty.

In the months that followed, when freezer space became available it quickly got filled up again. The food seemed to come from nowhere and everywhere. It came from fishermen who had caught too many fish, from people who didn't have enough freezer space, and it came as outright gifts.

A few weeks ago I was working in the front yard. A man, well dressed but looking as though he hadn't shaved for quite some time, approached me and said, "I'm on my way to Chicago to see about a job. I've been walkin' since yesterday afternoon, and I haven't had anything to eat since. I noticed you workin' out here. I'm very hungry. Do you happen to have any work for me to do to earn a dollar to buy a meal? I've been walkin' for a long time, but I'd gladly walk back to town if I had some money to buy something to eat."

I told him I didn't have work for him, but I would give him a sandwich and a cup of coffee if he would wait.

While he waited, I went into the house, locking the door behind me. I prepared a ham sandwich, placed it on a plate, and added some pickles and potato chips. I poured a cup of coffee and carried it outside to the waiting man. He thanked me and I returned to the house, again locking the door behind me, and watched him from the window. He gulped the food down, drank the coffee and went on his way.

I realize that helping strangers in this way can sometimes be, as the cigarette packages say, "dangerous to your health." However, I couldn't bring myself to refuse food to a hungry fellow human being. As I went outside to pick up the cup and plate the man had left on the porch steps, I thought of some of the information contained in the Edgar Cayce readings on economic healing. The freezer was starting to become empty again, and I wondered what the next food to appear might be.

That evening when Gene came home, he carried three large boxes into the house, one by one. As he placed the last one on the kitchen table I asked, "Did the Lord provide?"

"Yes," he replied, grinning sheepishly, "and our freezer runneth over."

# Venture Inward:
# Exploring the World of Dreams
###### ◆
## by Mark Thurston

OF ALL THE avenues available to us for the exploration of inner worlds, dreams are unique. The dream is a journey into altered consciousness which is available to every person daily. Because it is so commonplace many people may choose to belittle its importance when compared to other, more unusual methods of consciousness expansion. It is often our tendency to value too highly that which is expensive or rare; yet, if we are wise in our spiritual search we will appreciate that experience which is given freely each night. In our personal, inner search working with dreams is not just a starting point but continues to be a main vehicle of self-discovery.

One of the primary contributions of the Edgar Cayce readings on dreams is in clarifying the very nature of the dream experience. The following passage perhaps best summarizes the definition of dreams and visions. One should especially note that these are described as actual experiences of the mind and the soul. What we call a dream is only the recollection of that experience, and often our recall is presented in symbolic form. These symbols form a language of our dream life which is closely related to the experiences we have in our conscious waking lives.

**Dreams (for this body has many) come through the various channels as we have given respecting dreams. Dreams or visions are the subconscious forces of an entity while the conscious forces are subjugated, and the experience for the mind of the soul (or the subconscious) is often tempered by the physical or mental experiences of the body, and when such is the case these then are presented often in emblematical ways and manners. 302-3**

One basic assumption in these readings is that dreams are usually given for our instruction. Our dream life is usually more closely attuned to our needs for growth and development than are we in the conscious waking state. The lessons or forewarnings available to us through dreams are such that we might think of dreams as a school that we attend each night.

**The school is as of lessons which are gained through that projection of self into the subconscious forces, through which and from which the greater lessons and experiences of the universal forces are obtained for the physical study. 294-67**

**Dreams, visions, impressions, to the entity in the normal sleeping state are the presentations of the experiences necessary for the development, if the entity would apply them in the physical life. These may be taken as warnings, as advice, as conditions to be met, conditions to be viewed in a way and man-**

**ner as lessons, as truths, as they are presented in the various ways and manners. 294-70**

Dreams are a process that forms an important part of our spiritual growth. This process involves the activity of integration and cooperation—discovering ways of allowing various aspects of oneself to work together in harmony. We see this process active in dreams; the term used in the readings to describe it is "correlation." With correlation one is seeking to find a relationship between two elements. In terms of our dream life there seems to be a function whereby the subconscious mind seeks to find a relationship between activities of our conscious, physical selves and the purposes and ideals held within the soul. Correlation is used in defining three different types of dream experience.

**Dreams are as other mental conditions of the threefold nature, experiences of correlation of conditions in the mental body, or correlation of experiences of the mental or physical body, with the experiences of the subconscious forces of the body, or the reaction from physical conditions existent in the body. One should, then, in interpreting dreams, be aware of that causing such conditions, through same make the differentiation, that the experience may be applied in the daily life; for only through experience does an entity or being develop; for little may be learned save by experience of the mental or a phase of the mental forces of a body, or through same. 302-3**

One way in which we can understand the above reading is as follows. There are three different kinds of dreams. First there are dreams in which the mind of the soul is looking for relationships (correlations) between various ideas that are held within the mental body. Frequently these would be ideas from the previous day's activities. Secondly, there are dreams in which there is sought the relationship between physical or mental experiences of the day with the experiences or ideals held within the subconscious forces (i.e., the mind of the soul). And finally, there are also dreams that simply are the product of conditions within the physical body, such as an imbalance within the digestive system creating a nightmare.

If we use these distinctions as a starting point, we can begin to explore some of the specific dream interpretation tools found in the readings. There is no simple system for interpreting dreams. If we look at the entirety of the dream interpretation readings, we find dozens of possible approaches to dream interpretation. Some of the most frequently used or most potentially fruitful techniques can be described in terms of questions we pose to ourselves about a particular dream. These methods include the following:

1. What is the theme of this dream? We might call this interpretation approach the thematic technique. It is based upon the assumption that frequently the most helpful course of action to take in interpreting the dream does not so much involve translating the symbols but stepping back and getting an overall picture of what is taking place in the dream experience. In this case what we are trying to do is formulate a short one-sentence summation of the action in the dream. Usually with this approach nouns are replaced with general words such as "someone," "something," "things," etc. The following is a dream in which this approach seemed to be most constructive.

*(Q) "I dreamed of being at a party or dance and of meeting there a girl, whom I've met, a Miss . . . and with her a boy I've heard her speak of as George. Later it seemed that she was crying, saying that George wouldn't dance with her and was acting curiously, and she wanted to go home. It seemed that I assisted her in some way. I don't remember whether l danced with her or took her home, one or the other."*

(A) Again in this we see presented to the entity that satisfaction that is seen in service to others. For though those whom the entity may contact are of the casual acquaintance, or only known by name, the service, even as the Master gives, brings that understanding, that feeling of satisfaction to the entity, to the Whole, that nothing else gives. Service—Service. 341-12

In this case the key to interpreting the dream was not so much determining what George might symbolize or what dancing might symbolize but instead coming up with a short statement of a theme of the dream, for example, "being of service to someone I know only slightly." In this case once we have the theme we actually have the interpretation of the dream, for its point is that the dreamer needs in waking life to have more of an orientation of service to others. In this case it is not really necessary to interpret the meaning of the girl, of George, or the setting of the dream. The following reading is another example of using the thematic approach.

(Q) "Went into store and asked for 10¢ worth of jelly beans and they handed me just four beans. 'Is that all I get for 10¢?' I asked. They told me just four. 'Well, then, how much are chocolates?' I asked, thinking to buy them instead of the beans. 'Three for $1.00,' came the reply. 'Just three?' I asked. 'Three,' came the reply. 'Then you can keep your chocolates, too,' I flatly stated and walked out."

(A) This shows to the entity the inconsistency at times in self, as regards the various conditions that arise in the daily life, if the entity would but take the time to consider same from every viewpoint. For, as inconsistent as the prices are asked of entity, as inconsistent do many actions of self appear to others. 136-21

In this case the theme of the dream might be "something is inconsistent and unfair." Once again the key to interpreting the dream is not so much determining what the number "four" symbolizes or deciding what jelly beans represent but instead focusing upon the overall theme of the dream and the realization that in his waking life the dreamer has been inconsistent.

2. Is this dream a picture of the exact opposite of what I am doing in waking life? We might call this approach the compensatory technique of dream interpretation. It was first suggested by the Swiss psychiatrist, Carl Jung. Jung theorized that to a large extent the unconscious mind is compensatory in nature. That is, if we have gone to one extreme in our conscious waking life the unconscious will tend to awaken the opposite extreme in our dream life as if to try to strike a balance. It is probably unreasonable to suggest that all dreams are compensatory ones and yet there are examples in the interpretations given by Edgar Cayce that suggest that some dreams are of this nature. The following interpretation is such a case:

*(Q) Wednesday morning, November 25, 1925, at home. "I was sitting at a table eating but more than eating—was packing it in. There was chocolate cake and coconut cake and all kinds of sweets and goodies—and I just had a great time eating it all up."*

**(A) In this there is presented to the entity, in this emblematical manner and way, the forces that are at work, as it were, in the physical being of the entity. That to the physical is as this: To hinder the desires, to hinder those natural inclinations and those better developments, for the physical to manifest in the physical world those normal conditions of same, is to bring on self those condemning forces of the physical being in the physical health in the material manner, see? for as is seen, the entity recognizes in this the opposite from that being enacted in the daily**

**life, see? yet the entity sees that in this constraining of self these detrimental conditions in a fashion, physically, mentally, truly, are being brought to the body those conditions that bring detrimental effects. Then eat more sweets, see? Not in excess, in moderation, for with all things let them be done in moderation, in decency and in order, and in a way keeping to those truths as set in the way as has been set for the law as is known to the entity concerning that necessary in self to bring the best normal gift to the world of the position occupied by entity. Then do it. 136-21**

The background for this dream seems to be that the woman has gone on a very strict diet. Having once perhaps indulged frequently in sweets, she has now totally removed them from her diet. To her body which had become used to such foods she has gone to an extreme, and in the dream the opposite extreme is pictured. Edgar Cayce's interpretation "then eat more sweets, see" may seem unusual at first. However, his subsequent reference to moderation is entirely consistent with Jung's notion that our dream life is trying to direct us to a sense of balance.

3. Is it possible that ESP is operative in this dream? The readings suggest that in the dream state our subconscious mind can be in contact with the subconscious minds of others. There are dozens of examples in the dream interpretation readings where a person was given helpful, needed information about some other person through a dream. Such telepathic dreams have been well documented in laboratory research. Perhaps even more exciting is the possibility raised in the readings that we can actually have a dream for someone else. In the example below, a woman receives a dream message actually intended for her husband. To interpret this dream we must examine the question of how to understand the symbol of some other person appearing in a dream. As we begin to

interpret that symbol, there are at least three possibilities: The individual in the dream represents a part of oneself, the person literally represents him- or herself (telepathy is operative in this dream), or the dream symbol represents some other person. The last alternative is a subtle form of dream telepathy for which we frequently do not look. If, for example, I dream about John, I may be likely to consider that that dream symbol represents a part of myself that is much like John, or even to consider that perhaps this is a telepathic dream telling me something about John or our relationship. But the readings raise the interesting possibility that John may symbolize even another individual who does not appear in the dream. In the following example, the character of H.H. is used to symbolize individual [900] (who is the husband of the dreamer).

*(Q) Morning of September 20, 1926. "I said to H.H.: 'Don't be constantly apologizing to people. Write and present to them that you have written and then let them judge for themselves. Continue with your writing and present it. You will be successful in it—your writing will be a success.' "*

**(A) In this there is presented that which has often been in the mind of the entity regarding the writing, the studying, of one near the entity. This presented through that action or speaking part, as it were, to another individual, in the way and manner as is seen. That individual is as one close in mind and thought and would speak same to self, see? Then, as is seen, this brings that as the lesson: Continue, then, with that writing, that presentation, that as has been given to be given to others, for in same will be success, and let others think—let others present their criticism. Referring, then, to [900]'s writing, as is seen. 136-46**

Another form of ESP dreams is a precognitive or warning dream. The readings are full of such examples as are many other books written about dream interpretation. But perhaps of greater significance is a theory found in the readings that some dreams which appear to be precognitive or warning dreams are in fact simply made up by the subconscious mind to match some fear that we have consciously held. In one reading (136-82) there is an example of this condition. The dreamer, [136], did not want to make a trip with her husband to Virginia Beach. Her reluctance to go gave rise to a dream of their having an automobile accident on the way. In giving an interpretation of this dream Edgar Cayce suggests that it is not so much precognitive in nature but simply a product of the mind which did not want to make the trip. Of course, this is not to say that we should ignore warning dreams, assuming that they are simply the product of our fears or worries. However, neither should we jump to the conclusion that every dream which involves an accident or injury is a warning that such events are about to happen.

4.   What would have to happen in my daily life in order for the events in this dream to become a reality?

We might call this technique the hypothetical approach. Such an approach could be used to discover certain kinds of warning or precognitive dreams. This is especially useful for warning dreams which do not so much show the catastrophic conditions which may arise, but rather depict situations that would come to pass *after* the warned-of event. A simple example of this is Edgar Cayce's dream of being born in the year 2100 in Nebraska in a seacoast town. In one sense this dream is a warning about impending earth changes. However, the content of the dream differs from a warning dream in which the earthquakes and destruction are actually depicted. In this case we might ask ourselves what would have to happen in order for Nebraska to have seacoast towns. And we might come to the conclusion that this could be a warning dream about impending natural cataclysms in the earth's surface. Another example of this hypothetical approach to warning dreams is found in the following reading of Edgar Cayce. Here he is warned that unless he is careful he may soon die. The dream itself does not depict death but instead shows conditions that might be expected in the after-death state. The approach to interpretation in this case would be to ask what would have to happen to the dreamer in order for him to have experiences such as shown in the dream.

*(Q) Dream had by Edgar Cayce Sunday morning, Dec. 6, 1931: "I was a little boy again. Saw the fairies or elves I used to play with, and among them I recognized [341], [849], [419], and [295]. I seemed to reason with myself that they were just as real when I was a little boy, and they were still in the spirit world, as they are now in physical life."*

**(A) This, as we find, rather the warning to the body of those impending conditions in the physical forces of same, that might be turned into those conditions wherein the body would again assume rather the spiritual surroundings, or enter the spirit world rather than in the material forces of the body; and unless there is sufficient of those creations in the minds of those in material as seen, to hold those that are in the position of being changed, those in the spirit would make such holds or demands as to make the separation from the body—see? Hence the necessities that there be, either those that seen *make* such activities, or such thoughts, as to *hold* for *material* activity—else the *spiritual* activity would begin again. 294-128**

5. Does the dream bring me an experience which I consciously fear? As we come to value the importance of working with dream experiences, we must be careful that we do not assign to the unconscious mind the quality of infallibility or infinite wisdom. In fact many of our dream

experiences may only reflect conscious attitudes, conscious fears, doubts, or worries. An example of this is found in the following passage:

*(Q) "Dreamed that I could never have a child—that none would ever come to me—that I would never give birth."*

(A) **This again is a mental condition that is being carried through the entity's forces, and presents only that of the mental, for with the application of self in that manner of the law, as has been set by the entity's study and knowledge of same, through same would the physical condition be acquired and brought about. Hence the lesson that is necessary for the preparations for such a condition—motherhood, and as this is held the highest service to the Maker, and to the one held dear in earth plane, so is that spiritual development necessary that the entity gain that with which to give to that body, that will depend upon this body, physical, that training mentally and spiritually to gain and give the best in the physical world. This will occur. Child will be born. Necessary that these be carried out, however, as pertaining to the law concerning such; that is, of that as given by the lawgiver on the mount. 136-16**

6. Does the dream give me some clue about a physical disturbance within my own body? As seekers along the spiritual path, we may have a tendency to look to dreams for important breakthroughs and insights related to our mental and spiritual being. However, a large portion of our dreams probably relates simply to the physical body. In such cases, such as nightmares, the dream may be a product of general imbalances in the body and really have no further interpretation. On the other hand many of our dreams are offering us specific guidance about how we may better attune the physical. Sometimes the clues are very obvious, such as the following example in which a

particular part of the body (the abdomen area) is especially featured in the dream.

*(Q) Sunday morning, November 29. "I was going to swim from a rickety platform—very insubstantial in its structure. As I jumped in or tried to dive in, I made a belly whopper—i.e., landed on my stomach—it hurt."*

(A) In this we find there is brought to the conscious mind, in an emblematical manner and form, through physical conditions existent in the body, that which may be used as the lesson for the entity, see? for as the pain in the inmost portion of the torso gives rise to the emblematical condition presented, the entering the water, the desire to swim, to dive, the entering into those conditions as regard to motherhood—and as the body finds self in the attitude ready for that, the physical conditions or structure in which the body has kept self is not prepared in the manner as would bring the better conditions for the condition of that office at this time, see? and as this will soon occur, the body should take cognizance and be more sure of that position by and in self for this greatest of offices given to the sex—woman. [2/26 She had miscarriage. A son was born on 4/4/27.] 136-22

7. If this dream were a real experience what would I have learned from it? Apparently in some dreams the subconscious mind creates an experience so that we might come to a realization or awareness. In this case it is the realization or awareness itself that is the interpretation. Oftentimes there is little need to interpret the specific symbols within the dream. An example of this type of dream is found in the following passage. The dream presents a rather complicated discussion between the dreamer and others related to the stock market. If this had been a real experience, the lesson he would have learned would have

been to think twice before opening his mouth.

*Mrs. Cayce:* . . . *"Then we were on the train coming home, and [137] and [140] were with us. I said in answer to [140], 'She got mostly money for presents.' I interceded in my mind or made up my mind to myself to invest the money carefully and take the interest therefrom. [140] said: 'Why don't you buy some stock with it—you know what to buy.' That seemed to upset my plans and I said in reply, 'Yes, I could do that—maybe it's a good idea.' [140] said to [137]: 'Don't you know a good stock?' and I put in, 'Oh, I don't want that commission house stuff,' and then I was sorry for it seemed to reflect on [137], for [140] turned in a way half angry to [137] and said, 'Do you play commission house stuff?' [137] avoided the question and I wanted to be left alone to my own judgment to act for myself without receiving advice or offering explanations . . . "*

Mr. Cayce: . . . we find a correlation of existent conditions and those to be experienced in the body, mind and individual self of [900]. This, as we see, being a dream, and the wholly reaction in the subconscious forces, and is emblematical of that existent in self of the timidity of expression and the lack of the correct study of self before expressing self to others. Relating rather, as seen here, to all conditions in life, whether pertaining to the closer relations in business, in social, or of whatever nature may be considered.

Hence this is to be taken then in the manner in which the body may use same to bring self to the better understanding of self. Think twice before speaking of any condition. The body finds self under strain at the present time, pertaining to many different conditions and ways. Before answering, then, in any, as is shown here, be sure of the position the body takes in every condition presented to self. 900-49

8. Is this dream simply a rehash of the previous day's experiences? In some cases the readings did not offer a profound or insightful interpretation. In these instances the dream was simply described as the product of thoughts or activities of the previous day. Of course, we should not make it a habit to write off our dreams as simply a replay of things that have happened before. We must keep in mind that even an important dream will often incorporate ideas or individuals from the previous day's experience. However, if after a reasonable amount of time working with the dream you seem to have made no headway, it might be well to consider the possibility that this dream has no interpretation other than the possibility of a simple replay of recent experiences. An example is found in the following dream interpretation:

*(Q) Does the dream I had last night—regarding the opening of four eggs and chickens coming out—have anything to do with my physical condition?*

**(A) Rather as we find it has to do with that which was part of the experience in talking to some others just about two days ago, regarding chickens and their value in the experience of individuals in a home.** *Not* **regarding the body. 379-12**

These eight dream interpretation techniques do not represent the entirety of approaches found in the readings. They are, however, relatively simple, straightforward techniques that can be of tremendous value as we venture inward to explore the inner worlds of dreams. Especially as they are coupled with the use of ideals and meditation, they will lead to self-discovery. Through meditation we attune ourselves more closely with the highest ideal within. Such attunement will make it more likely that our dreams will reflect specific guidance for development and growth. And as we consciously work with ideals in our daily lives we are better able to apply the message of the dream. Of course, any inward venture must be coupled with an outer adventure. The real interpretation of a dream is what we do about it, not what we intellectually say the dream means. It is this balance of knowing within and applying without that is the key to our spiritual unfoldment. Dreams and their application can be at the heart of such a journey.

# Karma as Memory

◆

## by Bonnie Alt

ANY DISCUSSION OF karma assumes a knowledge of reincarnation, the belief that the soul of a man manifests in different human bodies in different ages, in order to evolve back to the perfection that it once lost. This theory embraces the idea that life is continuous, that there was a pre-existence of the soul before it entered the earth, and that the soul will continue to exist with purpose after the death of the body. With a perspective of reincarnation, we can see that death truly has no sting.

Many people do not like the idea of reincarnation because it gives them a responsibility. What is meant by this?

There is a law that we observe—whether we like it or not, whether we are conscious of it or not. We have read it in the Bible. We have seen it in the readings.

" . . . for whatever a man sows, that shall he also reap."
(Gal. 6:7)

"He who leads into captivity shall go into captivity; he who kills with the sword must be killed with the sword." (Rev. 13:10)

**Mind becomes the builder. The physical body is the result. 3359-1**

All of these expressions are telling us that our acts in one lifetime are answerable in the next. Technically, this is called karma, the law of cause and effect.

So, since our actions create reactions for ourselves, we are wholly responsible for whatever mess we find ourselves in. We can no longer blame the devil and claim he made us do it. Likewise, we can no longer blame God. Therein lies the responsibility.

**Ye that worry and are troubled, ye that are doubtful and fearful, who hath brought this upon you? God?** *God* **hath not at any time tempted man, but if ye will but accept it He hath prepared with every temptation, with every fault in man, a way of escape. 262-85**

Karma is a Sanscrit word meaning cause and effect. The readings do agree with this definition, but they enlarge upon it. *Karma is memory.* Many people think of karma as "debts"; but consider the following two extracts.

*(Q) What debt do I owe John . . . ?*

**(A) Only that that ye build in thine own consciousness. 1298-1**

**Each soul pays for his** *own* **shortcomings, not someone else's! 1056-2**

It is typical for us to recoil from the idea that karma is memory. Why? Because it prevents us from using karma as an excuse. Hugh Lynn Cayce has pointed out that many of us say, "I can't do anything about that relationship because it's my karma." "I'm paying a karmic debt" is another stock explanation for the turmoil we often find ourselves in. Yet, if karmic debts are something that we are literally going to have to pay for, why did the following reading admonish the individual to change his concept of it?

*(Q) Is there some karmic debt to be worked out with either or both [my parents] and should I stay with them until I have made them feel more kindly toward me?*

**(A) . . . What IS karmic debt? This ye have made a bugaboo! This ye have overbalanced within thyself! What is thy life but the gift of thy Maker that ye may be wholly one with Him?**

**Thy relationships to thy fellows through the various experiences in the earth come to be then in the light of what Creative Forces would be in thy relationships to the ACT ITSELF! And whether it be as individual activities to . . . thy father, thy mother, thy brother or the like . . . self [is] being MET, in relationships to that they THEMSELVES are working out and [it is] *not a karmic debt BETWEEN* but *a KARMIC debt of SELF that may be worked out BETWEEN the associations that exist in the present! And this is true for every soul.* [author's italics throughout] 1436-3**

What is this reading saying? One statement I feel it is making is that for any of us to claim that we cannot do anything about a relationship because it is what we call a karmic debt is *not* valid. According to this reading there are no debts *between* souls; your only debt is to yourself.

Of course, you have had previous encounters with the other fellow in other lives. And because of this, because certain individuals have helped engender certain memories within us, be they feelings of malice, impatience, stubbornness, or whatnot, these same individuals are the instruments needed to help remove these memories that are within us. Memories of a soul, yes. Debts between two souls, no.

Now, consider this extract: "He [Jesus] alone is each soul pattern. He *alone* is each soul pattern! *He* is thy *karma*, if ye put thy trust wholly in Him!" (2067-2) How can Jesus be our karma? This statement might have a clearer meaning if we substitute the word "memory" for karma here. We can now read it as "He is thy *memory* . . ." Now that's an interesting statement. It gives us one good reason to start changing the memories we are storing within. Essentially, we have two choices: either we can continue to create thought patterns based on feelings of retribution, revenge, etc.; or we can build memories of the Master Soul, Jesus, by applying His laws—doing what He found not grievous to do. This latter way need not be so difficult. But if we expect it to be arduous, it will be. "Be consistent, be persistent, be prayerful. Expect something to happen." (3779-1) Don't expect the worst. *Expect* His succor and " . . . put thy trust wholly in Him!" (2067-2)

"Come to me, all you who labor and carry burdens, and I will give you rest. Take my yoke upon you, and learn from me, for I am gentle and meek in my heart, and you will find rest for your souls. For my yoke is pleasant and my burden is light." (Matt. 11:28-30) The readings express the same thought in these words: "Karma is met either in self or in Him." (2990-2)

Meeting karma in Him, then, offers us an alternative to meeting our memories the hard way.

**. . . meeting those things which have been called karmic, yet remembering that under the law of grace this may not be other than an urge, and that making the will of self one with the Way may prevent, may overcome, may take the choice that makes for life, love, joy, happiness—rather than the law that makes, causes the meeting of everything the hard way.**

**For the self is constantly meeting self. 1771-2**

In summary, if you want to work with the idea that you owe debts, if you want to encourage your past-life urges and memories, you can choose to remain under the law of karma. But if you would rather live under the law of grace, begin by making your will one with the Way. **What ye sow, ye reap, unless ye have passed from the carnal or karmic law to the law of grace. 5075-1**

## What Is Grace?

Grace is a law—just as karma is a law. But grace lacks the sting that one can experience from cause and effect. It is God's love for man, His caring, His forgiving. How does one get under the law of grace?

Seven specific ways to move our lives from cause and effect to grace have been suggested. This transformation involves changing the quality of our lives and our attitudes. This is an important matter, deserving of serious consideration. Are you indeed willing to change your attitudes? Or are you one who feels that you are all right, that it's the other guy who needs to get in shape? Consider an observation made by Tolstoy: "Everybody thinks of changing humanity, and nobody thinks of changing himself."

If you acknowledge that there is room for self-improvement within you, then you can freely work under the law of grace. That you don't have to accept the negative consequences of your acts which have come back to you as karmic memories is another demonstration of the Father's love for you.

Let us consider these seven suggested ways of bringing ourselves under the law of grace:

1. Exercise righteousness

**What is righteousness? Just being kind, just being noble, just being self-sacrificing; just being willing to be the hands for the blind, the feet for the lame— these are constructive experiences. 5753-2**

2. Be joyous

**Not as one to be long-faced. For, the earth is the**

Lord's and the fullness thereof—in *joy!* Do not see
the dark side too oft. Turn it over—there's another
side to every question. Cultivate in self humor, wit.
Ye enjoy it in others, others enjoy it in thee. But too
oft it becomes to thee foolishness. *Know* that thy
Lord, thy God, laughed—even at the Cross. For He
wept with those who wept, and rejoiced with those
who rejoiced. 2995-1

3. Be gentle

And to do good, to be kind, to be gentle, to smile
even when in pain, to look up when others are even
tramping upon thine feet and give praise to Him in
the inner self, is that He seeks for. 815-3

4. Work with your ideals

For, there are those immutable, unchangeable
laws. These are oft termed in the material world
cause and effect, or—by some—karmic influences.
Yet none of these, if the ideal is set, should separate
the individual entity from the awareness of the Creative Forces' operation through its own experience.
3106-1

5. Avoid self-condemnation

Keep self unspotted from the world; condemning
not thyself, then, but rather leaving behind those
things that would so easily beset. Turn thy face to
the light in Him always and the shadows of doubt
and fear will fall far behind. 622-6

6. Be creative

For an individual entity, with all the attributes of
body, soul and spirit, is subject to the laws thereof;
and until individuals are in their thought, purpose
and intent *the* law—that is constructive—they are
subject to same. 1538-1

Then as the entity sets itself to do or to accomplish that which is of a creative influence or force, it
comes under the interpretation of the law between

**karma and grace. No longer is the entity then under the law of cause and effect, or karma, but rather in grace it may go on to the higher calling as set in Him. 2800-2**

7. Forgive

**For if ye would not forgive, how may ye expect to be forgiven? 633-5**

**. . . there may be forgiveness for those that err once; is there for twice, is there for thrice? Yea—though ye forgive, if ye would be forgiven! For that is the law. 5753-2**

"If you forgive a man his sins, they shall be forgiven to him; and if you withhold forgiveness of a man's sins, they are kept." (John 20:23)

You may be exercising some of these patterns some of the time. But if you aren't consistently following all of them all of the time, then you will have to admit there is room for improvement. Make it easy on yourself; or would you prefer to be like Saul, who rebelled against making his will one with God's? As the readings point out, " . . . if the entity or body becomes antagonistic to self or to those about self, it is only kicking against the pricks. For, know—it is self ye are meeting; not someone else." (1056-2)

The necessity of manifesting the Father's will as we deal with whatever conditions confront us is brought out in the following advice from the readings: " . . . these influences as indicated for the entity in its own application may not be dodged. There are no dodges for any individual. *Meet* them face to face!" (1150-1)

If we do all those things which Jesus did when He established Himself as a pattern, as a memory for all souls to follow, will it not naturally come about that our wills shall become one with God's? And isn't this what we should be working toward, not fighting against? This act, making our will one with the Father's, is referred to in the readings as "the escape" from karmic experience.

**As has been given as to what karmic influence is, and what one must do about same. Lose self in the consciousness of the *indwelling of* the Creative Force . . . through the *Son* of man! This is the escape, and what to be done about it! Lose self; make *His* will one with *thy* will, or thy will be lost in *His* will, being a *channel* through which He may manifest in the associations of self with the sons and daughters of men! 275-23**

So learn a new profession—become an "escape artist." Move to the law of grace.

# Universal Laws

## by Bruce McArthur

... TO HIM, TO His laws, must all come; the nearer we apply same in keeping with same, the greater blessings to self, the greater may be the blessings of self upon others. **2906-1**

Universal laws have been with us far longer than we can really conceive. The Edgar Cayce readings give a fascinating story of the beginning of man's understanding of these laws. According to the readings, the second ruler of Egypt began to gather together representatives—some 44 wise men of the "eastern and western worlds" (5748-2)—from all lands "wherein the human life dwelled at that period" (5748-2), and a conclave was held to study the first laws concerning man's relationship to the Higher Forces. The courts were held in tents and caves, and—most startling of all—this meeting occurred "from the present time being *ten and one half million years" ago!* (5748-2) The narrative further relates that the great problem of that period was the invasion of the lands by great beasts which were very "destructive to man's indwelling in many ways." (5748-3) Out of this conclave came the realization regarding the "first law of self-preservation in the physical plane attributed to Divine or Higher Forces." (5748-3)

**. . . force that gives man, in his weak state . . . the ability to subdue and overcome the great beasts that inhabit the plane of man's existence must come from a higher source. 5748-3**

Apparently now is the time for a greater understanding of these laws. In referring to the present, another reading concludes: " . . . there comes then the urge for the return of man's more perfect understanding of the divine [universal] laws . . . " (5748-4)

We are generally familiar with civil, criminal, and international law. Such man-made laws are established to keep and regulate order in designated areas. But what is Universal Law? We might define it as: Law that operates in all phases of man's life and existence, for all human beings everywhere, all the time.

An example of such a law on the physical plane is one with which we are all familiar—the law of gravity. This law satisfies part of the definition concerned with operating everywhere: Jumping off a cliff in California has the same impressive result as doing it in Peru! Also it applies to all human beings: The result is equally certain whether you are an infant, son, grandmother, or president. And, of course, gravity is effective all the time—it never rests.

Are there other characteristics of Universal Laws? The readings emphatically state that these laws are not subject to change.

**These are *unfailing*, in spiritual, in mental and in material aspects. These change not. They are *un-***

*changeable* laws. [author's italics] 3409-1

Then, what meaneth these laws? They are not merely statements or ideas, but are *immutable, unchangeable, eternal.* [author's italics] 2524-3

What are these laws? The readings mention more than 40 dealing with aspects such as relationships, forces, expectation, giving, judging, shortcuts, love, awareness, and many others, which could aptly be referred to as the laws of our lives. In this article we will consider those referred to most frequently in the readings, assuming that they are the ones with which we are most involved. However, we should realize that there must, in fact, be an infinite number of universal laws, for " . . . there must be a law to *everything*—spirit, mental, material. To be sure there is . . . " (1885-2)

Though you may have been unaware of these laws all these past years, is it important to study them now? After all, you do not have to study or know a great deal about civil or criminal law to get along in the world.

One of the great distinctions between man-made laws and universal laws is the fact that universal laws are so all-pervasive; they are operative in our lives at all times and in all places, in all of our relationships and in all of our activities. We do not have to break them to become involved with them. We are involved with them every day of our lives.

Universal laws have a unique characteristic: They always work, whether or not you believe in them or are aware of them. When you "break" the law by not complying with it, the penalty automatically becomes a part of your life. You do not have to be caught—you pay the penalty regardless! Conversely, in complying with the law certain rewards automatically come as a result. Therefore, it behooves us to study these laws to gain a greater understanding of them; then we can learn to use them more constructively in our lives. This process is effectively stated in the following reading:

**And as the development through the physical plane is to gain the understanding of all universal laws, the knowledge thus attained and made a part of the entity, brings the development . . . Hence the necessity of the given force as was said, "My son, in all thy getting, get understanding," and the ability to apply same. 900-25**

In fact, use and application of these laws benefits not only oneself, but others, as attested here:

**Man's development . . . is of man's understanding and applying the laws of the Universe, and as man applies those, man develops, man brings up the whole generation of man. 900-70**

Are we subject to these laws—or are they laws only of the universe? The readings give this answer:

**. . . so long as an entity enters into this solar system of urges, it is subject to the laws thereof. 3645-1**

But do we *have* to obey them? Have we no choice?

**. . . with the *will* man may either adhere [to] or contradict the Divine [Universal] law . . . 3744-4**

And if we choose to pay the price in time and make the effort to study and apply these laws, what will be the effect in our lives?

**For remember, there are immutable laws as respecting the mental and spiritual life. And these are they that live *on* and *on*. And in the material associations these are the basis of that manner in which the entity should act, should express itself. For it is in so doing, in sowing the seeds that are truth, that are life, that are eternal, that the source of happiness, peace and contentment arises. 1752-1**

With happiness, peace, and contentment as our goals, let's study our first lesson, our first law, for which we have chosen this title: *The Law of Us.*

**This is the first lesson ye should learn:**
**There is so much good in the worst of *us*,**
**And so much bad in the best of *us*,**
**It doesn't behoove any of *us***
**To speak evil of the rest of *us*.**
**This is a universal law, and until one begins to**
**make application of same, one may not go very far**
**in spiritual or soul development.** [author's italics]
**3063-1**

We could summarize it as:

*Speak No Evil of Anyone*

This law is so simple and the importance of applying it
stated so clearly, it would seem that little more need be
said regarding it. Yet if we would sincerely comply with
this or any other law, we can do so more effectively if we
have a thorough understanding of its meaning.

One way to achieve this understanding is to analyze
each word. For example, the first key word here, *speak*,
according to the dictionary, means not only to utter words
but also "to express oneself; to convey a message." Since
we are well aware that actions speak louder than words,
this law evidently refers not only to speech but to all ways
in which we express ourselves, even to our thoughts (if
we believe in thought transmission between individuals).
The other key word, *evil*, is defined as: "that which is destructive, corruptive, or fallible, whether from natural circumstances, or by human ignorance, error, or design; that
which is morally bad or wrong; wickedness; sin; that
which causes or constitutes misfortune, suffering, difficulty, or the like; woe; anything that is undesirable because
of its injurious nature or effect."

Some years ago, while attending an A.R.E. function in
which a number of talks was given, one speaker seemed
to be particularly unappealing in personality, inept in presentation, and boring in content. My thoughts were certainly "destructive" regarding him. After the talk I went to

get my tape recorder in the front of the room. I was amazed to hear someone sincerely telling the speaker how very much the presentation had helped him. This was clearly a case in which I had not seen the "good" in someone who to my mind was one of the "worst of us." I was certainly not complying with this simple law of "speak no evil of anyone."

Through analyzing a law by considering examples of it, we may begin to comprehend the extent of the law. This knowledge, however, creates a challenge for us, as expressed in this reading:

**It is not all for an entity, or a soul, to have knowledge concerning law; whether karmic law, spiritual law, penal law, social law, or whatnot. The condition is, what does the entity do *about* the knowledge that is gained. 342-2**

We are urged, then, to comply with the law, to apply it in our lives. How can we best do this? The readings leave it up to each one of us to determine that for ourselves.

**. . . there are some definite and immutable laws [universal laws] that the entity should consider . . . in its daily life and dealings with others . . . knowing that the answer to the manner of application must come within self. 2524-3**

One of the best ways to seek these answers from within is to ask yourself questions. For example:

1. Have I been applying this law?

2. Whom do I consider the "worst of us"? Is there anyone (family, neighbor, business associate, acquaintance, public figure, national figure, or group) about whom I have negative feelings'?

3. How am I expressing myself about him or them (by word, by thought, by action, by lack of action, by implication, by gesture, by other means)?

4. Is my expression in any way evil (destructive, injurious, etc.; see definition)?

5. If so, how can I best change this expression? A key to this lies in the question: What is the "so much good" in those I consider the "worst of us"?

As we try to comply with this universal law we can know we have help and support far beyond our own feeble efforts.

**... for, as is seen, in the compliance of the laws of the Giver of all good and perfect gifts, grace is commuted unto him who would seek to do His biddings, and places self in the hands of Him that gives life abundant. See? 900-253**

## DISCOVER HOW THE EDGAR CAYCE MATERIAL CAN HELP YOU!

The Association for Research and Enlightenment, Inc. (A.R.E.®), was founded in 1931 by Edgar Cayce. Its international headquarters are in Virginia Beach, Virginia, where thousands of visitors come year round. Many more are helped and inspired by A.R.E.'s local activities in their own hometowns or by contact via mail (and now the Internet!) with A.R.E. headquarters.

People from all walks of life, all around the world, have discovered meaningful and life-transforming insights in the A.R.E. programs and materials, which focus on such areas as personal spirituality, holistic health, dreams, family life, finding your best vocation, reincarnation, ESP, meditation, and soul growth in small-group settings. Call us today on our toll-free number:

**1-800-333-4499**

or

Explore our electronic visitors center on the
Internet: **http://www.edgarcayce.org.**

We'll be happy to tell you more about how the work of the A.R.E. can help you!

A.R.E.
215 67th Street
Virginia Beach, VA 23451-2061